Caitlin: your a legend
in the Hospital.
we all love ♡ ya ☺

Born to Save

Martin McHugh

MARTIN McHUGH

WITH JASON BYRNE

GW00383333

www.**HERO**BOOKS.digital

HEROBOOKS

PUBLISHED BY HERO BOOKS
1 WOODVILLE GREEN
LUCAN
CO. DUBLIN
IRELAND

Hero Books is an imprint of Umbrella Publishing
First Published 2022
Copyright © Martin McHugh and Jason Byrne 2022
All rights reserved

ISBN 9781910827505

Cover design and formatting: jessica@viitaladesign.com
Photographs: Sportsfile and the McHugh family collection

Dedication

To my father Johnny,
who made me the man I am today

To all those who have survived, are living
with or have passed away from cancer –
especially Linda's mother, Mary who lost
her fight during the production
of this book

Contents

« ACKNOWLEDGEMENTS »

IN SCHOOL, WE were often asked by the teacher to write a short story, but little did I know 40 years later that I would write my own book.

Thanking every individual would be impossible, because I met so many great people over the years. What can I say about my family?

Growing up on the farm showed me that hard work pays off. We always gave one another a listening ear or a shoulder to cry on, and we had lots of laughter. We always had one another's back.

My father Johnny always made sure I got to matches in the front seat of the car, or came home in the boot when I was covered in muck. It was really a tough time for me when he passed away in 1995, but the support from everyone in the locality really helped me through it.

I want to say a special thank you to my home club Aughnasheelin. We are a proud small parish, and we are there for each other through good times and bad. The club gave me huge support when I got cancer for the first time, and that really helped me on my journey to recovery.

I also want to thank Kilglass Gaels. Making new friends and playing club football in Roscommon was a new challenge, even if it was just for a year while working in the meat factory in Rooskey.

And Clonguish in Longford! I transferred to the club in 2003 and they accepted me as one of their own. Playing with a great team and great players really helped me to become a winner on and off the field.

A huge thank you to everyone I crossed paths with through Leitrim GAA. My first inter-county manager Eamon McGowan always had faith in me when others said I was too small to be a goalkeeper.

Special thanks to PJ Carroll who helped Leitrim win the Connacht under-21 title in 1991. He was ruthless on and off the field but the man got the ball rolling for great days with the county.

And the great man himself, John O'Mahony! Not only did he guide us to that famous Connacht Championship success in 1994, but he made sure we had the heart and passion to live like the winners we became.

I also want to thank Dynamo Rooskey FC, Longford Celtic FC, Longford Wanderers FC, Longford Town FC, Ballygawley Celtic FC and Merville United FC.

From playing under my first soccer manager, big Mick Quinn, to the current Republic of Ireland manager Stephen Kenny, they all helped me develop as a 'keeper and I made so many lifelong friends at those clubs.

Huge thanks to TTM Healthcare, who oversee my job at Sligo University Hospital. Their support through my own health ordeals with cancer was second to none and I have happily been working for the company for over seven years now.

Special thanks also to RTÉ's Damian Lawlor. After we did an interview about my playing career, he asked if I would consider writing a book and I didn't have to think twice about it.

Damien then mentioned Liam Hayes at Hero Books. A few days passed and, sure enough in late-2020, I got a call from Liam, and that was the start of it.

A young man from Donegal by the name of Jason Byrne had written a piece about me in the *Irish Sun*, and he was so excited to be asked to help me tell my story.

For nearly every weekend for months on end, we would chat about my life for a few hours… and now it has all wonderfully come together.

It was strange looking back, but a great laugh. From the bottom of my heart, I want to thank Jason and Liam for giving me the opportunity to write this book. I really hope that when people read it, they get a sense of laughter and hope through everyday living.

And, finally, to Linda, my wonderful partner. She has been by my side through thick and thin and always made sure I had everything that I wanted. Behind every man there is a great woman, and there is no doubt Linda is my rock.

Going to my appointments and being by my side through everything; she really helped me through some difficult times and decisions. You always make sure I am in good spirits and have a smile on my face.

Martin McHugh
March 2022

◄ ◄ ◆ ▷ ►

IN APRIL 2020, with the world on hold, two blank GAA pages faced us every morning at *Irish Sun* towers.

With no matches taking place we had to think outside the box, so flashback pieces became the norm. It came into my head to write something about the Leitrim team of 1994, so I contacted my great friend and GAA commentator Patrick McGill, who had covered the county with *Ocean FM*.

He sent me a number for their goalkeeper Martin McHugh with a beaming endorsement to go with it… and so this journey began.

We ran a two-page spread that weekend, but keeping Martin's story to 1,000 words proved impossible.

It had always been in the back of my head to do a book, and when Martin called me out of the blue later that year about doing just that with his own story, it was a no-brainer. His sporting achievements aside, Martin is a wonderfully inspiring human being. Helping him tell his story was nothing but a pleasure, and we are now great friends.

This is not just a story about sport, it is one about life and the many challenges it can throw at you. Martin overcame every single one of those challenges with his head held high, and he should be very proud of himself.

Martin, I cannot thank you enough for allowing me to tell your incredible tale and what was a daunting task at first quickly became months of joy – and thanks for sending me his number Paddy.

Huge thanks to Liam Hayes at Hero Books for giving us the opportunity to get Martin's story out there. His support and expertise throughout this journey were second to none.

To my great friends in the media who kindly lent me their advice – especially Damian Lawlor, Mark Gallagher, John Fogarty, Mark McCadden, Micheal Clifford, Paul Keane, Fintan O'Toole, Denis Hurley and Ollie Turner.

John Connolly's articles in old copies of *The Leitrim Observer* via the Irish Newspaper Archives proved to be a hugely valuable source of information when researching Martin's playing career, and huge gratitude must also go to John O'Mahony.

Not only is Johno a huge part of this story, but he was invaluable for tidying up so many nitty gritty details for this book whenever Martin enquired.

To my home clubs, Killybegs GAA and St Catherine's FC. My career as a forward did not go as planned in either code, but my love for sport was born in Fintra and Emerald Park where I made friends for life.

A huge thanks to my sports editor Ciaran Farren and all of my colleagues at the *Irish Sun* who make life incredibly easy and enjoyable. A special word of gratitude to my brilliant colleague and GAA correspondent Gordon Manning, who has been nothing short of incredible to work with and is an amazing friend.

His support over the course of the last year and a half has been massive. Thank you, Gordy.

There are too many to name, but thank you to my many close friends who were as excited about this project as I was.

To my family and especially my parents Kevin and Jacqueline – thank you so much. I am so blessed to have you both.

And, finally, to my fiancée Avril. I don't know where I'd be without you. Thank you for your never-ending patience, support and love.

Jason Byrne
March 2022

Prologue

**Leitrim Intermediate Football Championship Final
Sunday, October 8, 2017**

'THIS IS IT LADS!

'WE ARE ABOUT TO RUN ON TO THAT FIELD…

'AND BE GREETED BY 1,500 PEOPLE FROM OUR OWN PARISH!

'SUCK IT UP!

'DON'T LET THE NERVES GET TO YOU!

'THIS IS WHAT WE CAME HERE FOR!'

We're held up in the tunnel under the stand at Páirc Seán MacDiarmada in Carrick-on-Shannon, the home of Leitrim football.

Half of the county seem to be packed into the stand above us, waiting for what is about to unfold. We have a job to do… Leitrim Gaels are in our way.

I'm roaring at my Aughnasheelin teammates, because I can see the nerves starting to build. This is a time for composure.

Our manager David Casey has given us the team-talk in the dressing-room, but it went on a bit too long. So we've missed our allotted time to run out onto the pitch.

We've had to wait.

IT ISN'T IDEAL.

We've waited for this day for long enough. We were chomping at the bit to get out there and do battle.

We eventually arrive on the field to a huge cheer. I haven't experienced this for a very long time... and it feels amazing. We are ready.

There is no turning back now.

These are my own people... my own parish, all my friends and neighbours roaring us on for the 2017 Leitrim Intermediate Championship final from the stands as 15 of us go through our final warm-up... before standing together as one for Amhrán na bhFiann.

This day has been building up since we qualified three weeks ago... it seems like an eternity. The match just could not come quickly enough.

THE EXCITEMENT IS rife.

Flags and banners are all over our tiny village in east Leitrim, just over the border from Cavan... where everyone knows everyone else.

The club were champions without me in 2008, but haven't been in the final since. I won a Longford Senior Championship with Clonguish in 2009 against Dromard... the year I was sick with testicular cancer.

I was just too ill to play in that final, but I was part of the team and still had my role off the pitch. Even though I had lost my hair, and chemotherapy had knocked the stuffing out of me.

The legendary Paul Barden's last-gasp free won us that title by a point. That was after a replay! And he insisted I go and lift the cup with him.

In hindsight it was great to just be there.

But it still hurt that I couldn't play.

THIS IS DIFFERENT with Aughnasheelin.

I'm 47 at this stage of my life, training with lads over 25 years younger than me... fighting together for a county final... again!

And I'm going to be starting in goals.

THIS IS WHERE I grew up. The people are very close. We all know everybody else's business, but we are always there for one other in our little community.

The funny thing is, I had no intention of playing this season at all. I went down to the field to do a bit of training with the lads one evening... for the craic, as you do.

One of the selectors, Richie Fitzpatrick, asked me to help out with the goalkeepers and show them a few things. So I promptly obliged.

Dean Flanagan and Sean Mahon were the goalkeepers, and Dean was first-choice between the sticks.

I did a bit of training myself as well, just to gather a bit of fitness while I was there, and as the weeks went on…. f**k, I was really starting to enjoy it.

The bug was back… not that I ever lost it! I went to the games togged, with no intention of playing.

Before fate took hold.

DEAN GOT HURT in the first-half of a league game just two or three matches into the campaign, so next thing Sean – our second-choice keeper – was between the posts.

You couldn't have written it, but Sean pulled his hamstring.

I had arrived at the game to help the lads… not even as a third-choice keeper. Next, I was being told to warm-up.

'Will ye f**k off will ye…

'… it'll take me half an hour to warm-up!' came my snappy response.

There were still about 20 minutes to go in the game.

But in I went… and we won.

I PLAYED BETWEEN the posts for two more league games after that, because the lads weren't back from injury. Dean had a bad hip flexor injury. I was asked to hang around.

The fact that I was pushing 50 didn't seem to bother anyone else, but I was starting to get a bit nervous. Mainly because of the age-gap.

Still, I played the next league game against Fenagh… and we won again.

By then, I had realised the game had gotten so fast, and I had gotten incredibly slow. It was time to start extra training. I began pushing myself more and more.

It was no cakewalk. I found it really tough getting back to that level, and I really struggled. I often had to remind myself I was 47… not 27 anymore.

I had to just do what I could.

Then Richie, one of our selectors, said something to me when we were at the early stages of training for the championship, and it stuck in my head.

'Keep at it… the cream will always rise to the top!'

He knew I would get there. His words really lifted my spirits. Getting that buzz back was great. I still love going to training, even now … doing my thing, and that was all sparked from this big comeback in 2017.

My kick-out was always my big advantage, and I can pick out anyone with a kick up to 60 yards away to this day. I loved that people looked at me in action and said, 'Oh wow, what a kick-out!'… once I let fly.

WHEN I WAS with Leitrim in the 90s it was a different focus altogether, because I was working hard for myself to try and get that No 1 jersey against Thomas Quinn and Martin Prior.

I made myself Leitrim's first-choice goalkeeper, but that was county football when I was in my early-twenties. When we won the Connacht title in 1994, I was 23 going on 24.

This was intermediate club football with another 23 years on the clock. But I loved the buzz and attention as it grew all the time and I had an extra pep in my step at training.

Word started spreading at that point that I was back at it with my home club, and I revelled in the limelight. I always had done, whether it was with Aughnesheelin… Clonguish… or Leitrim.

People were looking at me, looking at this idiot at 47 years old trying to win a county title. But I just loved doing what I was doing as well… back playing in goals.

After a few weeks training the lads and *training* myself, I really started getting fit again.

The way the Leitrim Intermediate Championship is laid out, you go into a group, with four games followed by a quarter-final, semi-final and final.

We won all four group games, and Dean was back in the team after recovering from his hip injury. I could see he was under pressure, and he couldn't really handle it well.

He made silly mistakes, but we got away with them.

I was there to help him, so I would speak to him at half-time – telling him to relax and take control. But it's easier said than done.

The last match against Fenagh was a dead-rubber because we were already through, but we wanted to go through the whole championship unbeaten.

Dean was under pressure in that game, and we were losing by two points. His kicks were going astray, he was making silly errors and, next thing, I was told to warm-up again as the management lost patience. My old competitive streak had long returned.

I knew this was my chance.

It was only the group stage, and we were qualified, but this was it! I was doing my warm-up on the sideline… jumping and leaping as usual.

THEN I GOT this sudden nervousness across me, because this was still a championship match… and I was pushing 50.

I only got around 12 minutes to prove myself and, as I arrived into the goalmouth, I said a little prayer to whoever would listen.

I fired one monster of a kick-out to Conor Cullen, who caught it and stuck it over the bar. And we scored again… to win 3-9 to 2-9. We still had our unbeaten record. I was in goal and I never looked back.

IT WAS TIME for the quarter-finals. It was do-or-die knockout football. We did just enough to progress against Mohill's second-team, thanks to Gavin McWeeney's late winner.

The semi-final was against Carrigallen's second team, who were a good side, but our heads were away with the birds again. We really struggled.

An early blitz of 1-5 made the difference in a 1-16 to 0-10 win, but the result was not a fair reflection. It was a below-par performance.

We luckily scraped through.

THE FINAL BECKONED… this was it.

Really deep, at the back of my mind, I knew we were in a good position to win despite our big quarter-final scare and a shaky enough display in the semi-final.

But we still had to prepare, and I had to keep my own head down because I'd been in this position before.

Every day in the life of a goalkeeper, someone is breathing down your neck waiting to take that jersey off you. That never changes.

We had a good management team behind us, training was serious. Everything we were doing was at a very high standard.

For a lot of the lads, this was their first final. They looked up to me for those few weeks given my experience.

But I had to keep my head down. I had to work harder than anyone because of my age... make sure I kept my place for the big one.

And tick that box with my beloved home club.

SOME OF THE training sessions were really tough.

Tough on me, in particular. But I got huge encouragement from the lads. We all pushed and drove each other on.

Training for goalkeepers is a lot different now compared to when I started playing football. It's not just... 'Kick the ball at me and I'll save it!'

Dublin legend Stephen Cluxton has changed the game for goalkeepers forever, and everyone in the country is constantly trying to match those standards.

During the season I was also doing a bit of coaching with Castlerahan's goalkeepers in Cavan. I really put Ciaran Daly and Jamie Leahy through hell over there, but really enjoyed it.

We worked on their reflexes, kick-outs... and their heads.

But all the while I had to do the same for myself.

Between juggling that and working so hard to stay fit for Aughnasheelin, it was a savagely tough few months.

I would get the lads to take shots on me... so I had to dive left, right... get up again and repeat it over and over... for a few minutes to keep myself sharp and on my toes. There was literally no time for rest at this stage.

Sometimes, I'd be winded from jumping a few feet in the air to make a save, and crashing to the ground again on my shoulders.

I was pretty well juiced by the end of it! Then I would practice kick-outs; not just kicking it long and hoping for the best. Those days are gone.

It's all about finding a teammate, going long or short. Winning your own kickouts is now paramount. Sometimes you need motivation to do better. For me, it was the spotlight and the attention I was getting. I had always loved it.

I used that to my advantage.

THE *LEITRIM OBSERVER* got involved in the build-up.

And, in the middle of one particularly gruelling session our club secretary

Shirley Sammon said the *Irish Independent* wanted to interview me. They were looking for players over 40 still going at a high level.

There were plenty of lads around the country my age, and even older, playing club football, but there was a bit of a spotlight on me. I had beaten cancer.... twice. And I just wanted to keep playing the game I love so much.

But I had to keep a level head through all of these distractions, and focus on beating Leitrim Gaels. They had been knocking on the door for a few years… and they actually won it in 2018. That's how good they were!

Castlerahan, who I had been coaching, made the Cavan senior county final and it typically fell on the same day as our match. But my focus was only in one place.

AS I AM roaring at the lads in the tunnel, I am nervous too.

I'm nervously focussed, if that makes sense.

The game goes according to plan, but we made a few mistakes as usual. We win a penalty and miss it… and they kick a few bad wides too. It's tight.

Leitrim Gaels cop on to my kick-out strategy and I adjust, but I can still feel the nerves filtering through the team.

Our forwards are missing simple scores… and our backs concede silly frees. At half-time we are 0-9 to 0-5 ahead. I keep my mouth shut and stay focused. Our manager David does all the talking.

MIDWAY THROUGH THE second-half, and we are ahead by three points. Our work-rate really went up. I can feel the excitement building inside me.

I know we are on the verge of winning.

But I tell myself out loud to calm down. With 10 minutes left, another surge of excitement filters through me.

'Jesus, we are going to win it!'

Then I am telling myself to calm down again… before the nerves come back. It is a vicious cocktail, and it comes back to bite me.

I am standing over a kick-out… but I have nobody to aim at.

Leitrim Gaels have every man out in front, and I am getting ready to take the kick. The ref blows me up for time wasting!

The lads on the sideline are going absolutely mental.

Luckily, we manage to clear the ball.

ANOTHER KICK-OUT!

Cormac Sammon is running from the stand side of the pitch, right across to the other side and I hit him on the move… and play the ball right into his chest.

He was a good 60 yards away!

He turns and plays it into one of our forwards… the ball goes over the bar. It's near the end of the game. The Gaels start losing the head, with time and the scoreboard against them.

They are going for their first title, but the cracks are starting to appear as we close in our first since 2008.

Our playmaker Barry McWeeney gets a lot of hassle and the Gaels are taking the mick at this stage. Gareth Foley is the referee. He's a good mate of mine. We had a little chat before the game.

It had no bearing on the result, but you never know when a decision could go your way when the result hangs in the balance.

THINGS ARE GETTING heated.

I roar… 'WHAT THE HELL WAS THAT?!' after a particularly heavy hit on Barry McWeeney.

I don't know if Gareth hears me, but there are people at home eating their dinner in Carrick who definitely might have. Barry gets his free and we send it over the bar to go two in front once more.

We kick another wide.

But we win the kick-out. Now there is more argy-bargy.

I think Gareth has enough of all this s***e.

He blows for full-time. We win by two points… 0-12 to 0-10.

I fall to my knees. I cry like a baby.

It all just comes flowing out… between beating cancer twice… training as hard as I did with my age and body firmly against me.

You put so much energy into one game, especially when you reach a final. You have all the preparation leading up to it… getting the head right, and staying focussed.

You know you have the work done. It's only a matter of going out onto the field… and doing it.

It takes a big toll on the body and the head to do all that.

EVEN GOING BACK to 1994, I was that man in the middle of the goalmouth being swamped by people getting all the claps on the back when we conquered Connacht with Leitrim… for one of the biggest upsets of all time.

Between that famous day and this one, the raw emotion of winning something major really takes over.

When the final whistle went, all of those emotions from those nerves and excitement came pouring out in floods of tears.

And most importantly, this is my first Leitrim Championship medal after all those years. I won a lot with Clonguish, but this is Aughnasheelin.

I am not the only one crying.

For our little village, this means everything… and the whole parish is out on the field. People are so proud of what the team has done. And what I have done.

I need no reminding that my father Johnny is looking down on me as well.

Daddy died in 1995 and he was football to the core. He would have loved this, but he is definitely looking down from heaven with a smile on his face.

It is such a proud moment for the team. But what I have gone through personally makes it so much more emotional.

The celebrations tonight will be wild.

It's another unforgettable day in my life as a goalkeeper… a 'life' that began in the schoolyard over 40 years ago.

PART ONE

'Who have we for goals'

Hardwork was part and parcel of every day on the farm for us as children and as you can see (left) I started young! And a proud moment with my dad (right) in 1994 with the Nestor Cup for company.

I realised from an early age that goalkeeping was my destiny – here I am with the Aughnasheelin under-16 team, long before I got it into my head to always stand in the back-row with the 'giants of the team'.

« CHAPTER 1 »

I FELL IN love with the ball straight away at school.

We were all mad for football, and lunchtime at Aughnasheelin National School just couldn't come quickly enough every day.

We would walk a mile to get the bus to school, down at the old forge every morning. The school only had three teachers but there was lots of fun, football and laughter. I took to it like a fish to water.

From fourth class onwards, I was always chancing my arm to play in the games with the older lads. Despite my persistence, I was always turned away but my time would come. Once you got into fifth class, you graduated to that sacred part of the yard where the serious games took place… from then on there was no place to hide.

It was just us lads at the start, going at it in games of slides in either gaelic football or soccer that never seemed to end, and we didn't want them to.

Before long, the girls wanted to get involved, so it was us against them in battles of the genders.

EVEN BACK THEN, I was a goalkeeper.

It wasn't because I couldn't play out the field or I wanted to be picked, or because nobody else wanted to be in goals. I just knew that if I could make a save or help to win a game, I could be a hero.

But me being *me*, I wasn't happy with the lack of work I was getting and I wasn't content with just standing there all the time during these one-sided games between the sexes.

I wanted to have an impact and be in the thick of the action, so I put in my transfer request and went to play in goals for the girls.

It was great craic and even then, I was a bit of a charmer, chatting up my new teammates! But I had a competitive edge that would never leave me.

Winning came first, so finding a girlfriend had to wait and, suddenly, I had gone from an idle figure in those games to a very busy man.

We started winning a few games on that girls' team, and even then I could kick the ball long from my hands, so we got the odd goal.

As time went on, the matches got more serious, and there always had to be a winner before we very reluctantly returned to class.

We had a small break late in the morning, and then half an hour for lunch. Most of the lads ate their food during the first break, so as soon as the longer break came you were straight out to the yard for the game and didn't have to worry about wasting precious time eating.

Out in the yard, a lad called Francis McTeague was playing football with us one day. He was a real farmer with no interest in sport, but he was great craic and a real character. This day when he was playing he was taking on two jobs at once. He was running around after the ball and making an effort, but at the same time he was picking at something in his pocket.

'What the f**k is in your pocket?' I asked, thinking it was probably sweets and I might get one off him. He had his sandwich in there, and he was picking away at it while playing the game at the same time. A ham sandwich out of the pocket of his trousers. For his sake, good thing there wasn't any jam in there!

ONE DAY IN particular, one of the lads was bearing down on me ready to score and I said to myself... *No way.* I was going to stop him by any means necessary.

So I dived down at his legs and sent him flying, tearing the arse out of my trousers in the process. Mrs. Dolan, our teacher, caught a glimpse of my heroic dive to thwart the opposing attacker, and roared, 'WHAT DO YOU THINK YOU'RE DOING!?'

I just told her outright that we were winning and I didn't want him to score. It was that simple in my eyes and my duty as a goalkeeper, but she wasn't impressed and the look on her face would have stopped a clock.

We spent a lot of time in the graveyard across the road to get stray footballs, and I was often the one deployed to get them even though we were forbidden to leave the school grounds during the day.

Any time Micheál Jordan, the headmaster, caught me I was forced to stay in the classroom for the rest of the break, but that only happened twice because it killed me! Sitting inside those four walls, you could hear the games going on outside, and it was the worst form of torture.

Sports day every year at school was huge. The whole village would turn up at the old field in Aughnasheelin for the craic and to watch all of the races and everything else that was going on. I was red raw useless for running when I was in national school, and always finished the races nearly last! But as I got older and my body developed and I got better at football, I always won those same races.

The football didn't stop when I got home from school either, but we had work to do first. I grew up with my father Johnny, my mother Breege, my brothers JJ, Pete and Leo, and my sister Marianne.

We'd help with the cattle or take in the turf and there was always something to be done around the house. We all pitched in.

WE LIVED ON a small farm where every day jobs had to be done around the house 24/7… rain, hail or shine.

If there was a job to do, we had to do it… even before school. We could be digging ridges for the spuds, going to the bog or taking in hay. Looking back now, it definitely made me strong both physically and mentally and provided me with a great work ethic for life.

We didn't have time to make up excuses. We just did what we were told. That's the way it was then, working like a trojan to get everything done so you could go and play football for the rest of the day.

AS THE TROUBLES raged in the north, and Dublin and Kerry were at one another's throats on the pitch, life in 70s rural Ireland was happy but centred around working hard and keeping food on the table.

When the work was done, I would be out in the field kicking the ball after the grass was cut and gathered…myself and my brother would just kick it over and back to each other… *forever.*

I would practice kicking the ball from a cut of rushes off the ground, but little did I know how important my makeshift tee would be later in life for getting distance on the ball.

Anything would do for a set of goals, from buckets to long sticks planted into the ground… so my brothers could take shots on me and push me to the limit. As I got older, watching the 1982 All-Ireland final between Offaly and Kerry made me want to be a goalkeeper even more.

Whenever the All-Ireland final was on the telly, daddy would close the curtains in the kitchen so we could get the best view of the screen. I remember watching that game as if it was yesterday, as an 11-year-old. Kerry were raging hot favourites and everyone felt they just had to turn up at Croke Park to collect Sam Maguire, but Offaly had other ideas.

People always remember Seamus Darby's late goal to win that game in front of Hill 16, when Mick O'Dwyer's Kingdom were denied history and the famous five in-a-row against all the odds. That goal is still played time and time again on the telly nearly 40 years later. But for me, it was Offaly keeper Martin Furlong saving Mikey Sheehy's second half penalty. That was my memory!

Darby's goal naturally gets all the limelight, but Furlong's save was another huge moment in that game. As Eugene McGee's Faithful won their All-Ireland against the head and every aspiring footballer pretended to be Seamus Darby, I said to myself… *I want to be a goalkeeper…, I want to be like Martin Furlong.*

To me, he was the man and the real hero.

BY THEN I had started playing for the club under-12 team down in the old field in Aughnasheelin, called the Shreheen. And Pat Cull was our manager.

There were no dressing-rooms; we just togged out under the bushes. There was a little river beside the field too which claimed many a football, and a lot of the lads would go in there for a dip after a game to cool themselves down.

At my first training session, we were all spread around in a semi-circle and Pat said we were going to have a game, but we needed a keeper.

'Who have we for goals?' he asked.

With about 20 of us there, all fingers pointed at me. It was usually the chubby fella who went in goals, but I was delighted because I knew that's where I belonged. I had potential and I never looked back. At training we played games amongst ourselves, or practised kicking the ball over the bar. It was as simple as that in what were much simpler times.

My father went to most of my games from an early age, and he would often bring some of my friends with him. The pitches around Leitrim back then were in awful shape – full of bumps and humps, and they were all fairly mucky.

I remember one time at our old pitch, I was wearing those iconic yellow Mikasa gloves with the black dots on them. Those big old gloves never let me down and I never left home without them.

A ball came in low and stopped dead in a massive puddle of water. I dived in on it, and was covered in pure shite from head to toe. That didn't bother me, but I think it bothered the auld lad. When he saw me walking back to the car looking as if I had a mud bath, he cleaned me off as best as he could with old rushes and grass from the side of the road.

He wanted to keep his beloved car clean from my muck, so he made me get into the boot for the journey home.

After that, he had a brainwave on how to keep me clean for matches. He got me a pair of blue tracksuit bottoms with straps on them that went over my shoulders.

They looked like something that Big Daddy or Giant Haystacks would wear in a wrestling ring back in the day, but I thought I'd be lovely and warm and dry with my new attire… and that my days of travelling home in the boot of the car would be over.

In the next game, we were playing against Fenagh in their old pitch beside the handball alley. It was a wet evening, and as usual the goals were flooded with a few inches of water – there were no games called off because of bad weather in those days.

But that didn't bother me. I had my new bottoms and I would be nice and warm… sure I was sorted! The game was on and before I knew it, another ball came in low and hard and I was called into action with my new clobber ready to go.

The ball stopped dead in the middle of a puddle of water, again.

So, I dived on it, got up and cleared the danger. Next thing my lovely warm blue tracksuit bottoms with the straps were absolutely saturated. The blasted thing was hanging around my ankles, and I could hardly move with the weight of the bloody water that all of the material had soaked up. My legs were like cement... it was horrendous.

Then I got so cold, I couldn't feel my fingers. I was going to be the first Leitrim man ever to develop frostbite in the middle of the summer. Something that was supposed to keep me warm and dry now had me drenched, freezing cold and moving like a snail. The bottoms were weighing me down badly, and the top part meant to be around my chest was hanging around my ankles. It was ridiculous, and I can't imagine how I looked to the people watching the game, including my dad.

From that day on, I never wore tracksuit bottoms in games or training. Nothing ever covered my knees on a pitch after that, apart from a few scars. But daddy meant well, and he was always a great support to me in every walk of life. He had a blue Hiace van... HIT52, and he used it to bring a few of us to training and matches whenever he could. Not everybody around that time had a car, so the van became our unofficial team bus.

He never gave me advice or tried to show me what to do, but he was always there to bring us to the games and give his full support. Just him being there meant the world, and looking back now, it was just marvellous to have that support.

One time we were down in Carrigallen's old field, and I was in sizzling form and making save after save. One of their forwards got so frustrated, he roared, 'Will you let in a goal, for God's sake!'

I hated missing training, and one day in particular I learned my lesson when it came to time-keeping. We had a few jobs to do at home, and the clock in the house said it was 5pm. We had a match at seven. Content with the time I had, I went off to get my work done, and when I came back in the clock still said it was 5! The battery inside it was stone dead... and it was actually five minutes to seven. I raised the alarm and we rushed to the car in a complete state of panic. Mammy brought me down and the match had started when we arrived. I was so pissed off, and cried and cried because I wasn't playing.

I know it sounds silly because it was only a game, but it shows how hooked I was on GAA from such an early age. I was beyond upset.

Pat put me on in the second-half and we lost, but I was never late for a training session or a game ever again. From then on if training was at 7, I was there at 6.30 and poor time-keeping has been my pet hate ever since.

ON THE FIELD, I just loved making saves, people clapping and saying, 'Well done!' Not every game was perfect, and I did make plenty of mistakes like most goalkeepers do. It can be horrible when you make an error because the buck stops with you, but moving on immediately and kicking out the next ball is vital.

There were no goalkeeping coaches back then either, so I was largely self-taught in a way.

When a game began, away you went and the trust was placed in you to do your job and perform. But I developed my own standards as a goalkeeper, and began teaching myself how to do better any time I made mistakes.

By the time we got to under-14 level, we had to be able to kick the ball off the ground and that's when all my practice off the cut rushes really paid off in terms of power. It gave me plenty of height and distance to my kicks in the meadow at home, so I was well able for it out on the pitch.

There were no kicking tees then either, but I was cute about it. Using my heel, I would make a nice round lump in the mud for the ball to sit into when the referee wasn't looking, to give me the perfect launch-pad for my kick-outs.

I often made two or three of them in case one was trampled on during the game, such was my ingenuity in the goalmouth. It was a great way to get some height on my kicks… and a good thump behind them. I got under the ball and just hoofed it down the field, hoping that one of my teammates won his battle for possession after that.

I loved diving, and was able to dive to my right no problem, but I struggled with diving left. Over time playing games, I got better at that and put a lot of work into it.

I was never really thinking about playing for Leitrim back then; it genuinely hadn't really crossed my mind. Just playing club football for my local team gave me a real sense of love for the game at a really young age.

FOOTBALL WAS CENTRAL to life for a lot of people in the village. There was no pub, so a lot of visitors and neighbours used to call around to houses to play cards, including our own.

They'd call down, tell a few stories and play poker. There was no real money involved – just match-sticks and no more than an old two pence or five pence coin would ever be on the table. It was another simple social outlet, but there was a great sense of community because we were such a small parish.

Everyone knew everyone else and if someone died, you knew who'd arrive at the wake house first for the drop of whiskey; people would go and gather until all hours.

Every weekend we went to mass; everyone in the village did. I always said my prayers, but I always waited hard on the priest's local notices at the end of it, if we had a game. He always announced if there was a match on, urging the locals to go and support us. It gave us a sense of belonging, and I used to fill up with pride during that moment because we felt like heroes in our little village.

Everyone in the village and across Leitrim had a farm in some shape or form. My father was always up at sunrise ready to go at it, especially in the summer. During the winter he fed the cattle before he went to work in the pig factory in Rooskey.

We had great neighbours down the road called Packie and Kathleen Harvey. They were brother and sister and lived in a really old cottage. She did the house work, and he worked the farm. Packie was a really old-style living farmer. He'd go down to dig the ridges for the spuds, but would never leave the field until the job was done. He'd have the sandwich with him and his tea in a glass bottle... no flask! When I was growing up, they were both well into their seventies, but farm life was all they knew.

If we were down helping them, we'd go back to their house after the work was done and poor old Kathleen would have tea ready and sandwiches with big lumps of butter hanging out of them. You didn't want to offend anyone, so you took a bite and quickly had a drink of tea to wash the lump of butter down your throat. Since then, its been no butter for me!

It was hard slogging, but it was the way we lived. There was no technology like there is now. If you had a job to do, you had to do it, and there were no questions asked. But once the jobs were done, we were never stopped from going to football training or a match. You worked hard and played hard... it was all we knew.

I wouldn't have changed it for the world.

« CHAPTER 2 »

ALL I WANTED to do was play football, and it didn't matter to me if the match was in Timbuktu, Aughnasheelin or on the moon.

The sport was my drug, and I came to realise that from a very young age during those epic playground battles with my schoolmates. When I started secondary school at St Felim's college in Ballinamore and prepared to enter my teens, my love for sport only increased – but I was getting fed up with education and the classroom.

Just like in national school, the football matches at lunchtime were a great distraction and the highlight of my day – despite the change in venue, uniform and personnel. Playing games for the school team gave us a great chance to dodge classes for a few hours, and I signed up as soon as I arrived.

I played soccer and basketball there too, to spend as much time as possible away from the books and my teachers. Second year dragged on for me, and I just completely stopped enjoying it and really had enough. I could just feel I wasn't gaining anything from education any more, and I could not see that changing as I began to mature. I was just so heavily concentrated on sport, nothing else really mattered.

In the end, I only lasted three years at St Felim's and in 80's Ireland dropping out of school before sitting the Leaving Cert was very common anyway. It wasn't frowned upon like it would be today. This was a time when having a job still meant more than having a decent education.

When I was in second year I secured a summer job in Hanely's pig factory in Rooskey. It was where my father worked, and it was great because I learned more about life there than I thought I could in any classroom.

We were up at 6.30 in the morning for the 45-minute drive to work. The first job I had there was making boxes for the meat, and sometimes I would pack the meat into them myself. The money was good, and once I had a few pounds in my pocket I was happy enough to drop out of school and just count my wages every week instead!

Being the people they were, my parents asked me to do one more year and sit the old Inter Cert exams, just so I had that extra bit of paper before I waved my educational endeavours goodbye. Once I had those exams over me, myself and my folks would continue the conversation and see where I was at.

Eager to strike a deal, I did what they wanted and went back to school for one more year. Looking back, it was the right decision as I knew my days in the classroom were numbered and the great escape was on the cards.

What turned out to be my final year at St Felim's was hectic. Club underage football started up again in early 1986, and it was a new dawn for Aughnasheelin in the form of a new ground with dressing-rooms and all, and everyone was thrilled with our new state-of-the-art facilities.

TIMES WERE MOVING along nicely across Leitrim in those years, and some of the other clubs in the area all had new pitches too and the standard of club fields gradually improved.

And my ability as a goalkeeper really started to grow too. The great writer Cormac McGill said in the paper one week that I had the 'reflexes of a cat'. I definitely purred a bit reading that, because it was a strong indication that I was progressing nicely.

My kick-outs were improving all the time in terms of how far they went, which was all that mattered back then, and people around the club started to take notice of my potential. I hadn't even been taking my own kick-outs until I reached the under-14's because I was small and the power just hadn't come yet. One of our outfield players, John Reynolds, took them before that because he had an old 'bull-toe' as we used to say, and he could really drive the ball up the field.

But I kept practicing and was soon a match for John's bullets, and when I showed the managers what I could do, I finally had the green light to take them myself.

By the time I was 16, Tom Costello came to the house. He was a neighbour and a great clubman, and wanted me to come and play adult football with the Aughnasheelin junior team. But he had to get permission first, so when he asked daddy if he would let me play, my father was hesitant because of my age.

He knew I was progressing well, but this was a men's team full of old dogs twice as old and twice as big as me. He eventually agreed, and I remember Tommy giving my father his word that they would protect me. Tommy himself was going to be my trusty full-back, so that helped daddy agree. Tommy was around five feet nine, with a beer-belly on him, but he would do his best to keep me out of harm's way in the small square.

The standard was low; it was basically just a bunch of old lads playing football. I had developed into a decent 'keeper, and I was fairly strong and had a good kick-out.

Johnny Reilly had been in goals for Aughnasheelin – a really hardy buck who took no prisoners when he came for a ball. He was getting on a bit, so they needed new blood but Johnny had some wise words for me as he was passing on the baton.

'If you ever come for a ball,' he advised, 'come out with your elbows pointed out and your knees up. Any on-coming forwards won't be long pulling away.

'They'll know you mean business.'

TOM CAME INTO the dressing-room with a few of the old characters, like Adrian and Joe McGirl. These were real men – hefty, hardy f**kers who took no nonsense! If you could have painted their faces, you would have… because this was a bunch of old farmers ready for war.

Some of them were handy enough footballers as well, and here I was at 16 going out to play with the 'big boys'. I was nervous, but I got on with it because I had no feckin' choice. It didn't phase me to play with these men, but it wasn't like now where you win a free if you get a belt on the shoulder.

You needed to get a kick in the head to win a free back then, and to say things often got physical is an understatement. We were playing Mohill one day, and I saved the ball but was tackled on the ground as I went down with it. It was a hard hit, and I was down for a few seconds seeing stars. I remember Tom Costello, Brendan Reynolds and one of the McGirls coming in and charging on top of the fella who tackled me to teach him a lesson.

'You don't hit a gasún on the ground like that, you f**ker!'

Next thing, there was an awful row, but I knew I had that protection from my full-back and the rest of the lads as promised. My father was always included in that protection gang too, even though he was only a spectator. Against Gortletteragh one time, he came in and started choking a player who had sent me flying!

A ball came in over the top, and came to their corner-forward Mickey Doorigan. I ran out and caught the ball, and with my momentum I side-stepped him. He left a leg trailing out by accident, so I tripped over it and went flying. I tumbled on to the ground, and daddy ran on to the pitch and grabbed Mickey by the throat.

Tommy arrived on the scene again, this time to calm my father down! It was a complete accident, but just another day in my footballing apprenticeship.

We won absolutely nothing with the club back then. The standard training was just a few games, and maybe a few laps to get the heart going. We had some decent players, but we were never any good as a team. We never lacked for effort, but always fell short when it came to big results. That was our downfall.

All the while, I was really developing my own skills, and coming up against all those older lads really helped that. The likes of Brendan and Mícheál Sammon, Pat McTeague – these were lads I looked up to.

Some of the others didn't have much skill. They loved playing football, but they were red-raw. If they didn't get the ball, they got the man.

LOOKING BACK, NOT winning anything with those lads didn't matter because I learned so much more. Soldiering with them, you quickly went from a boy to a man, because you had little choice. It was sink or swim in those mucky goalmouths. And I loved it.

I did well in my exams and got three honours and three passes, but I still dropped out of school as planned, because I just couldn't wait to get away. Life now was my job in the factory – and I stayed there for the next 14 years.

I was cleaning, packing, pushing pigs into the pen and doing anything I could get my hands to, throughout my first formal career in the outside world. The factory made me permanent that September, and I was thrilled. There was a lot of knife work involved, and you had to be handy with a blade.

The pigs would be delivered on a Monday, and would be slaughtered and cleaned out that evening and pushed into the chill freezers. The next day, they were wheeled out again and cut up into different joints. Over the years, I learned all the ropes and knew everything there was to know about pigs!

So, I developed my skills and became a trainee butcher. I even progressed to showing other lads how to use the knife, because I had mastered it.

My father was a head butcher in there and whatever he had in his blood, he passed it on to me. I was cutting the ham legs off the side of the bacon and I was fairly good at it. I trimmed fat from the meat, and cut the joints into different parts to perfection. Then I progressed on to boning joints… we were given a quota of 200 to do each day.

I was that good, I often finished two hours before it was time to clock off, but sadly I couldn't just up sticks and leave.

I usually left a few joints on the table so if a supervisor came in, he would think I was boning away… and I would usually lend a hand to some of the lads if they were 20 or 30 joints behind to help them catch up. As the years went on, I became a floor supervisor with two other colleagues. We were in charge of over 150 people.

It was a big factory that offered huge employment, and a staff of over 300 or so offered that extra bit of responsibility and was a crash-course in management… and people skills too. But most importantly, the factory was great craic to work in, especially because a lot of Roscommon people worked in it.

Jumping ahead, I remember playing for Leitrim against the Rossies in a National League game when I worked there.

On the Friday before the game, the Roscommon lads were all boasting away in the factory… and we beat them. They were fairly quiet on the Monday morning… and I just stood there smiling from ear to ear, as the other Leitrim lads in the place let them know all about it.

You got home at 5pm after work and the chores for my parents were still there to do, followed by training if it was on. Between working there, on the farm and playing football, the summers flew by.

I WAS HAPPY out, especially on Friday evenings when all of my attention turned to the game at the weekend. Because there were no pubs in Aughnasheelin and a lot of the other small villages in Leitrim, going to matches was a really big social outlet for people. There were always a few stragglers there early, and a lot of local news and wisdom was passed on at football matches.

The pitches had no stands back then either – it was just old wire around the field. You played away, and beat the heads off each other and, if it rained, the supporters got wet.

One evening, when we were working in the factory, myself and my father set off for the bog because the weather had been good and dry for a few days and it was key to strike when the iron was hot. We nipped out of the factory early to tend to the turf, which I was delighted with. There was a nice crust on the turf, and a few clouds were starting to gather overhead but we paid no heed. We went ahead footing the turf; which meant placing five or six sods upright and leaning against each other.

It was back-breaking work, but a nice change from the factory and we had to get ready for home, but the clouds continued to spread and get darker and darker. All of a sudden after a couple of hours into it, the heavens opened. Daddy being *daddy*, he decided to stick at it because we had already got so much done. He was of hard stock and insisted a drop of rain would do us no harm; so, we stayed on for another few hours as it pissed out of the heavens.

We were absolutely soaked to the skin and our wellies were filling up with water when, eventually, we made for home.

In those days, hot whiskey was the ultimate way of fending off the flu, so I jumped into the bath while my mother got the hot ones ready for us.

I sat in the tub sipping on my drink, with cloves bobbing across the glass, for around 15 minutes. I got out of the bath and stumbled around the room a small bit! I never fancied a drink after that, but at least I never caught the flu so the medicine did work. Another time, one of the lads had a pint in front of him one night in the pub, and I took a sip from it and I knew then for sure it really wasn't for me.

Even in 1994, when the whole of Leitrim was going mad after winning the Connacht title, I was the only sober person in the county, and stuck to the Club Orange when everyone else went buck-mad on the booze.

Smoking was a big thing back then because nobody knew of the health risks associated with it like we do now. You'd skip the odd class in secondary school to meet up with the lads and have a fag down in the forest behind the old tech in Ballinamore.

Sometimes, we'd sneak a fag or two from daddy's Sweet Afton box, but they were very strong and you really felt it after smoking one of them! The odd time, me and one of the brothers would chip in and buy a packet of smokes, and go for a 'long walk' as we called it, around the area to have a few puffs and talk nonsense.

Before long, my father found out about us smoking and this meant trouble. He was a heavy smoker himself, and told us we were at a crossroads. We could keep at it and go around the place huffing and puffing like him, or give them up and live a healthy life.

I still kept smoking for a few weeks after that, but I could find my lungs getting heavy so I completely stopped it, thankfully. Even though I didn't drink, it never stopped me from having a good time. We used to get a bus down to discos at Kelly's in Mohill, Freddie's in Ballinamore or even down to Belturbet in Cavan.

We always went out on Saturday nights after our work was done at home and on the farm. The odd time we'd go to a pub first, and play pool if there was a table in the corner to get the craic going. I loved rock music, and was a bit of a head-banger, but I always waited for my time to come for the slow-set so I could ask a woman to dance at the end of the night.

After a disco you might get the odd bag of chips, but other than that it was always mammy's dinner at home with homegrown spuds. We ate pheasant sometimes, as we used to do a lot of shooting around the land. We had a good pointer dog, and that helped!

My mother would pluck the pheasant and cook it for dinner that evening if we shot one, so we were quite literally putting food on the table.

WEEKLY LIFE WAS normal, otherwise – until one evening after a training session in 1986. Seamus Prior walked into the dressing-room. He was a prominent national referee at the time and a great Aughnasheelin man. Seamus was heavily involved in our club at the time training different teams, and he said, 'Martin, you are being picked up tomorrow evening. You are going to the county under-16 trials!' I got a huge shock, because I had never once thought of inter-county football. Playing for Leitrim genuinely never crossed my mind.

It wasn't a big ambition or anything because I genuinely never expected it, and I was just happy playing for my club.

Maybe that attitude helped my cause for a call-up, because I was never wrapped up in any obsession to play for the county like other lads were.

Patsy Wrynne's bus was going to collect us at Michael Moran's post office in the village, and Patsy took no shite on the bus! His son Adrian used to drive as well, and that's when the craic started because we had a bit more leeway with him.

We were often more focussed on having the craic on the bus than on representing the county or who we were playing. Ray Logan, Gerry Cox, Enda O'Brien, Pauric McLoughlin and myself would all be on the bus and it's a miracle we never got arrested for acting the mick on those journeys.

We just didn't care – we were getting away from home and were let loose for the day. Ray was liable to do anything during our spells of newly-found freedom. When we got on the bus at the post office, we went off on a big loop around Leitrim across all the different parishes to pick up players... and head for Carrick-On-Shannon. We went into Ballinamore, Aughawillan, Drumreilly, Cloone, Aughavass... and on to Carrick with a full load.

I was nervous because I didn't know what was ahead of me and the prospect of stepping up a notch does throw you. At the first session there were nearly 40 players there, and I was picked to play in a few trial games before the panel was trimmed down for the Father Manning Cup. I made the cut.

We came up against Longford, and Enda Flynn was a magnificent forward for them. Later in life when I was ill with cancer and won the 2009 county title with Clonguish, he was chairman of the club and over all of those years he never scored a goal on me, which I still slag him about!

We never won any serious competitions, but it was nice to be selected for the county and get a first taste of playing with the pick of players at my age group. I had a bit of pride because somebody had spotted what I could do as a goalkeeper for my beloved club, in the midst of my father's glare and those old farmers ready for war.

« CHAPTER 3 »

IN 1987, I naturally progressed onto the Leitrim minor panel and a few lads from the under-16 squad came with me. After you got the call, it was time to impress at the trials. The drill was the same… and you just hoped that you made the cut when the panel was trimmed down for the season by the management.

But I still didn't know what it was all about, or even if playing for Leitrim was that high on my agenda. I might have been a working man and all that, but I was still so young. I was just enjoying my football with the club, and I genuinely wasn't thinking about Leitrim under-21 or senior teams.

The game was a hobby to me. Thankfully, it always was and that mantra never led me astray.

Others were nervous at the trials and probably had the ambition of playing for Leitrim in their heads for a long time, but I just relaxed and went with the flow.

It was obviously the start of a new adventure, and the spark for what was to come for the guts of the next decade. But I was happy out, just playing away with the Aughnasheelin minor and junior sides with my old pals from school, and the old dogs for the hard road, who loved taking lumps out of each other.

AT THE SAME time, I was quickly developing a new confidence in myself as I headed towards my late-teens. I was a working man, and my ability on the pitch was continuously catching attention.

I had been in goals for the Leitrim under-16's, and just presumed I would be selected for the minors too without putting any pressure on myself or thinking too much about it. At that age, it was probably the best way to be.

Peter Mallon was first-choice 'keeper before I eventually succeeded him, but my only minor championship match for the county ended in a 3-11 to 1-7 Connacht preliminary round loss against Mayo in 1988.

They destroyed us that day in Ballina, so my career at that grade was not exactly something to shout about… and the less said about it the better.

The training with the Leitrim minors wasn't severe or even that organised, not like it would be later in my inter-county experience, and that's a pity because we did have some great young players.

All it ever was, was just a game with a few drills and the odd bit of running. We trained twice a week, had a game at the weekend. That was it.

Looking back, standards could have been much higher and there were definitely some opportunities wasted as my days at minor level came and went with nothing more than a whimper. Our year was over on May 21.

Around that time, I continued my path into adulthood and moved out of home. Dad wasn't working in the factory then, so I used to drive down every morning myself. I soon got to know everyone in Rooskey. I soon moved just to be closer to the factory, and I wanted to spread my wings and fend for myself.

It was nice to get a bit of independence. If you made a mistake at work or something went wrong at home, it was on you – and that sense of responsibility made me stronger in myself.

The standards at underage football in Leitrim never really changed or improved until PJ Carroll took over the seniors and under-21's in 1989.

And the difference was night and day.

THAT'S WHEN THE shit really hit the fan for football in the county – either do the work, or f**k off! PJ raised the bar, and the work he did laid great foundations for Leitrim for many years to come. His insistence on managing the under-21 and senior teams was a pivotal factor in raising standards and giving young talent a clear pathway to senior football for the county.

We got to the Connacht under-21 final in 1990 against Galway, after beating Mayo 0-6 to 0-5 in the 'semis' with Martin McGowan in goal as I looked on from the bench. We had a team of good, strong players but Galway beat us 0-9 to 0-5 in the showpiece with the likes of Sean Óg de Paor, Tomás Mannion and Kevin Walsh in their team.

I ended up crossing paths with all of those lads for the next few years in some great Leitrim victories, but they would all go on to lift Sam Maguire with the Tribesmen in 1998 and 2001.

I was being the usual joker and idiot on the bus after that game. John Connolly from the *Leitrim Observer* was on board and we were all a bit down in the dumps on the journey home from Pearse Stadium in Salthill.

PJ Carroll was up at the front with his selectors, and John was down the back with us so I started cracking jokes and he laughed the whole way home.

John is originally from Dublin but has been a huge part of Leitrim sport for over 20 years covering the lot for the paper, and I was playing the comedian to lighten the mood in the wake of defeat.

Even though we lost that final, it was progress for Leitrim football and PJ knew we could take the next step with what we had, so the whole dogged procedure started again for the 1991 campaign.

We had to do trials once more so everyone started off from scratch, but I knew in the back of my mind I was probably going to be first choice 'keeper this time around because Martin McGowan was overage.

But I still had to work hard and keep my head down to make sure it happened, and there would be no more cracking jokes on the bus.

In the meantime, I switched clubs to make life a bit easier for myself too. I'm sure they were silently unhappy in Aughnasheelin, but I transferred to Kilglass Gaels in Roscommon just to save the driving home for training and matches when I was living in Rooskey. But I was still a Leitrim man through and through, and we had a strong under-21 panel again with the likes of Ray Logan, Declan Darcy, Padraig McLoughlin and Pat O'Callaghan. This time, the training was severe and there was no room for messing or slacking off.

IF I THOUGHT I had escaped St Felim's college, I had to think again because that's where we often trained.

There was a hill at the side of the school pitch and we had to go around the field, up the hill, across and down again… 20 times.

It was chronic stuff but standards were being set and we had to meet them. Back then goalkeepers trained with the rest of the team and I had to run every yard.

On a hot dry evening, the pitch used to be like a road, and I had blisters on top of blisters. PJ ran the absolute s***e out of us!

The training consisted of games, running… and more running, and I never questioned why I had to do it as a goalkeeper. With PJ, you did what you were told and kept your mouth shut for your own good, but he really got the best out of us.

We played Westmeath in a challenge match and the ball came over the top.

I decided to come out, as their corner-forward was running for it and there was no sign of any of our defenders.

He got there before me, but there was pressure on him and he kicked the ball wide. PJ gave out f**k to me!

'Where the f**k are you going McHugh?! GET BACK TO YOUR GOALS!'

At half-time he reminded me about it, and did so again after the match! He said if I ever did it again, I could stay at home.

If you did something he didn't like, he told you all about it and reminded you about it again in front of everyone so you learned your lesson. Everything had to be one hundred percent perfect with no mistakes. That's how PJ wanted it… sheer perfection and nothing less.

From then on, I really raised my own standards, because I knew I was at the top now and I had to stay there. This was county football… sink or swim.

My kick-outs, catches and saves all had to be perfect and that was the mantra with PJ Carroll and the Leitrim under-21's that summer.

We were fit, strong and everything was done right. Nobody else ever believed we could do something except for us, and that's all that mattered. The atmosphere was just different with PJ in charge. You had to s**t or get off the pot, there were no half-standards anymore. This was to be taken seriously.

Training was just so severe, and the level was so much higher than it was when we were playing with the county under-16s and minors. The difference was actually night and day. Those sessions, before he arrived, were hugely made up of a few drills, some sprints, a game and then home, with nobody putting too much effort in. But it was just a different kettle of fish with PJ.

He was a stickler, and even told us what time we had to be in bed at the night before a game.

With the frame of mind he had us in, if he told us to be in the cot at 10pm we made sure we were tucked up at 9.55pm.

It all had to be done his way, or you were told to go home. He trained us like soldiers before the championship, and we were as fit and strong as we ever were as a result.

We had built up serious stamina, and it would stand to us. The laps at St Phelim's college and the blisters were the making of us both on and off the field.

It made us mentally strong, and when the pressure was on, we were able to handle it. We knew we had the work done, and we were not going to throw in the towel… for anyone! You always kept going until the last second and that final whistle, as long as that jersey was on your back.

BECAUSE PJ WAS in charge of the Leitrim senior team as well, sometimes the likes of myself, Ray Logan and our under-21 captain Declan Darcy were brought up to their panel to make up the numbers at training, if lads were away or at work.

Again, I didn't know much about the Leitrim senior team or who I was even training with – I just went with the flow and did what I was told without any fuss.

I remember they were playing a challenge game against Sligo in Annaduff, and I was on the bench. But it was in the back of my mind that things were progressing well for me.

Here I was sharing a dressing-room with the elite players in the county… with the No 16 on my back. And I twigged that there was a big future there for me in county football, if I wanted it.

We had a good few players on the under-21 squad who stood out. Brian Prior in front of me was a great defender, then you had Darcy and Gareth McWeeney. Despite that, PJ was a great man for focusing on the panel as a whole rather than making us play through individuals, which was a huge part of who we were and why we achieved what we did.

We had a togetherness as one, and that's why we became Connacht champions that year. As I already said, nobody gave us any hope apart from ourselves.

We were straight into a semi-final against Mayo on April Fool's Day in Carrick.

They had a game under their belts and had impressively taken care of Roscommon in the quarter-finals by seven points. But we had the last laugh and pulled off our first big shock to beat them in the last four.

I made a vital save 11 minutes into the second-half to deny Colm McManamon a certain goal. It was the turning point in the game when all was said and done.

I went down to my weaker left side to block the shot heading for the corner, and after I made the save I could hear the supporters in the terrace shouting with approval… 'WELL DONE McHUGH'

That was my first little Martin Furlong moment, and one of the reasons I wanted to play in goals – to hear my name being shouted for doing something right.

That was it from day one back in the schoolyard… and here I was living the dream in goals for Leitrim in a big championship match.

A young forward from Ballintubber called James Horan was one of their main men up front, but he only scored a point. We blew them out of the water.

Horan would go on to have a stellar senior career for the county and also lead Mayo to all those All-Ireland finals as manager, but he didn't get a sniff against us. We actually scored more goals than points that day, and the final score was 5-4 to 0-14. Goals win games and Pat O'Callaghan got three of them for us, but keeping a clean-sheet was vital and we powered into another final.

But I never concentrated on the opposition, and only focused on us. Playing Mayo, Galway or anyone – I didn't care who we were coming up against. My own standards, performance and the result were paramount and nothing else mattered after that. If we conceded goals, the buck stopped with me and I had to be seriously on the ball with as little distractions as possible.

I always found that if I thought too much about the individuals on the other team, it affected my own focus on the game and that can be costly.

But one of the few times that changed was ahead of the All-Ireland under-21 semi-final against Tyrone, when everyone was raving about a certain Peter Canavan and his brother Pascal in the build-up. I'd soon find out why, but we'll come to that.

In the meantime, it was great to be in another Connacht final against Galway. They were going for five in-a-row.

But losing against them the year before gave us an edge, because we were determined not to let that happen again and suffer that pain of defeat in a final.

It wasn't often Leitrim had a big shot at provincial glory and we had to make every one of them count. There would be no more stupid jokes on the back of the bus from me, unless the cup was on board too.

My mantra was to focus on my own performance. This was a high-level championship final, so I had to keep my head down, stay in the zone and work hard even though we only had six days to get ready for Galway.

That was my approach for league and challenge games, and I wasn't going to move away from that now. We trained again on the Tuesday night before a light session on the Friday before the game.

After that, we went for a meal and team-talk at the County Hotel in the middle of Carrick-On-Shannon. PJ says to me, 'You better be in bed early tonight, McHugh!'

Because I was living on my own in Rooskey, he was afraid I'd be out gallivanting, but sure enough I was tucked up nice and early and got plenty of sleep... as if PJ was keeping watch outside.

THE STAKES WERE high, there was silverware on the table and we knew what it was like to lose... *and going home on the bus cracking those jokes.* That was all to hide the elephant in the room but it was time to put things right.

There were no nerves as I went through my usual routine, staying focused on my own performance. I would go into the back showers before throw-in and just kick the ball against the wall and catch it again 20 or 30 times to get myself revved up.

We went out and warmed-up together. I practiced a few kick-outs and, before we knew it, the game was on.

It was incredibly tight to start off, but I hadn't too much to do because my defence was just so organised. However, I had to concentrate on getting a good distance on my kick-outs to ensure we kept possession, or at least aim for a teammate who could win his own ball and keep it away from the sea of maroon jerseys at all costs.

By this stage my kicks had developed really well, thanks to my own craftiness in building those little divots and makeshift kicking tees in the mud at the corners of the small square and along the 20-metre line in front of me ready to go.

Those good long kicks were my advantage from the age of 16 the whole way up. For the first one, my legs were like jelly and I must have taken about nine steps instead of my usual five before pulling the trigger.

When the next one came, I told myself to calm down, took a deep breath and let fly after five steps. Calm was restored.

Back then it was route one stuff… just hit it as long as you can and hope one of your teammates wins his battle and comes away with the ball.

I always let out a little grunt when I kick the ball, and that day was no different. I still do it today, and it does work! It gives the ball that extra bit of venom to make it go further.

I can thank PJ for my grunt, because I can still hear him roaring at me if I was standing over a kick-out.

'KICK IT OUT!

'KICK IT LONG!'

I'd be wound up a bit from his barks, so that's where it came from and it never left me.

If you have nothing to do in front of you in terms of saves, you have to still keep your defenders on their guard. To this day, I roar and bark like an idiot during games and that one was no different. It kept my defenders on their toes, and nobody was allowed to wander two yards from his man.

If you weren't touching him, you weren't marking him as far as I was concerned.

I pissed the lads off no end, because I would not shut my mouth. People in the stand were even telling me to shut up, and I then would shout even louder. That still happens nowadays too.

But we pulled off a 1-7 to 0-9 victory in front of our own, as Colin McGlynn's goal proved vital. Galway's Ja Fallon needs no introduction and was a vital part of their All-Ireland glory in 1998 and 2001.

He was their rising star at the time but, just like Horan, he only scored a point. The Tuam Stars man would turn into a superstar in his senior career, but he never got the chance to properly test me that day in Carrick, thank God.

I hadn't a clue, anyhow, who he or any of his teammates were at the time. They had Niall Finnegan and Sean Óg de Paor as well. When I look back on old match reports now, I see I faced some serious legends.

But this was our day, and the only legends were us.

We were never going to lose that final in front of our own after leaving Salthill with nothing the year before. My family was there, including my father, who went to all of my games and it was a very proud moment for the McHughs of Aughnasheelin.

So many people flooded onto the field at the whistle in wild celebration, and the craic in the dressing-room was on another level.

The Galway chairman Jack Mahon came in and congratulated us, wished us well and said we… 'were a very lucky team'. His comments made a few headlines at the time because it came across as sour grapes. He was obviously disappointed, but he spoke from the heart and I think a few people maybe took him up wrong. He was genuine and knew we were deserving winners.

When you think about it, we were lucky in the Mayo game for sure because of the save I made… and they kicked some bad wides.

That week, there was a picture on the front of the *Leitrim Observer* where I'm holding the cup with Pat O'Callaghan, who was immense for us again, and his shot led to our goal.

Pat was from Manorhamilton, and he was a good tidy player but we never saw him play for Leitrim again after that season.

County secretary Tommy Moran is in the middle of us in the photo and we're both kissing him on the cheek. It was our first title at that level for 14 years. Over 2,000 people were at the game, to savour history in the making.

The lads belted out *Lovely Leitrim* in the dressing-room, but I didn't know the words. I haven't a note in my head, so I kept it low-key in the corner of the room and joined in for the chorus.

Even now, looking back at the pictures and what we had achieved for the county, thank God I won what I did when I see how starved Leitrim have been of success since then.

It's hard to believe that victory was over 30 years ago now, and it remains our second ever under-21 provincial crown. The other was in 1977… and the next one might never come at all.

I didn't know what was to come with the seniors, but winning that Connacht under-21 title was such a huge achievement for us and laid the foundations for the next few years at senior level and becoming a genuine force in Connacht at last.

Going home to my family and seeing the pride they had in us winning a provincial title was massive. I really felt that from a personal point of view.

We were top of the pile after beating Galway and Mayo, and I hadn't conceded a single goal. I just kept concentrating on my own performances – it worked a treat and I could not have asked for more than that.

Despite what you might think, there were no wild celebrations after that. We had a meal after the game and went our separate ways. It was all quite sensible, but that's because it had to be.

THE SEASON WAS far from over.

We had three weeks to prepare for an All-Ireland semi-final against Tyrone.

PJ ensured we didn't lose sight of that – he didn't want to undo any of the dogged work we had put in up to this.

The game was fixed for Brewster Park in Enniskillen and we knew we'd be up against it. All we heard about was this Canavan fella and his brother Pascal lighting up their attack, and how they were very impressive Ulster champions who'd make a serious tilt at the All-Ireland.

But PJ was still adamant we were going to beat them. He had us like lions in the dressing-room, ready to go out and tear these lads from the north apart.

We had all these plans for man-marking some of their forwards but, in hindsight, this was like Longford Town coming up against Real Madrid. It was chalk and cheese.

We were so delighted with our Connacht title that All-Irelands hadn't been on our radar, but that's what Tyrone were aiming for.

After that day, it was no surprise to me when Peter Canavan went on to become an icon. He had blistering pace, wonderful feet, incredible accuracy... he simply ran riot against us.

There were no more clean sheets for me because he scored 2-3, and they won 4-13 to 2-7 to march into the decider against Kerry.

Tyrone totally outclassed us in every position on the pitch and Peter Prior missed a penalty, which summed up our day.

The way he ran up to kick them was very easy for 'keepers to read, but to make things worse he failed to hit the target and put it wide.

Tyrone, on the other hand, were just lethal, and it was a bad day at the office for me. The way they moved the ball was so sharp and quick, and they created space with ease to pick off their scores. It was no surprise that they went on to blitz The Kingdom in the final too and it was a huge reality check for us.

We had put so much energy into winning Connacht and beating Galway and Mayo, but these lads were different gravy.

Even though they were a clear class apart, I was gutted. I always have my own high standards, and even when we won games and I conceded goals, I was disappointed afterwards.

I could have made 10 saves in that game, but the fact that we lost and I shipped four goals was so disappointing after keeping a clean-sheet in the Connacht Championship… and the scoreline people read in the papers couldn't be changed.

I'm my own harshest critic but, thankfully, the *Leitrim Observer* felt otherwise, and John Connolly wrote: *Looking for good performances on Sunday might seem out of place, but players like Martin McHugh, Peter Prior and Donal Smith all played their hearts out in a lost cause.*

Indeed, for a period of the first-half, McHugh's ability between the posts was all that kept Leitrim in the game – the wonder of it is how the Aughnasheelin man isn't No 2 'keeper on the senior team?

It was all a stepping-stone, but my whirlwind Leitrim career to date and the intensity under PJ had already taken a toll.

I already needed a break from football as my 21st birthday approached.

PART **TWO**

Johno

John O'Mahony, brought our level of professionalism to an even higher level when he took over from the great PJ Carroll as team boss. Johno (above) enjoys his moment in the sun after we had defeated Mayo to claim the Connacht title. PJ, and Johno especially, guided me to reach my fullest potential as a goalkeeper (right).

« CHAPTER 4 »

AFTER LOSING TO Tyrone, we were still regarded as legends because provincial titles were just so rare in the county.

That's when people started viewing me as the lad who was in goals for the Leitrim under-21s who won the Connacht championship. But I took a break for the year in 1992 just to get away from it, because the amount of training we did with PJ was huge and had taken a toll. I needed to do something different with my own abilities, and in hindsight that little break from football was the making of me, even though I did transfer clubs and went back to Aughnasheelin.

On top of that, my son Sean was born in February 1992.

WHEN THE GAA wasn't on, there wasn't much to do around Rooskey at the weekends and I used to head down to the small gym in the village just to give myself something to pass the time and keep myself in shape.

There was a small soccer club in the area called Dynamo Rooskey, and I worked with their kit-man PJ McGuire in the factory. He said they were mad for a goalkeeper, and he asked me to play.

It was a different outlet, and it was nice to go and play another sport. The good thing about playing soccer with Dynamo was you didn't even have to train – you just turned up on the day of a game. No laps, no hills… no blisters!

Their base was a field off a main road with a cowshed as a dressing-room, and a telephone wire ran across the middle of the pitch. It was a classic country soccer club.

Most of the games were on Saturdays during the winter months, so even if I had games with Aughnasheelin (or Leitrim) I could juggle both. Sometimes they did clash, but not too often, thankfully.

I was introduced to the manager Mick Quinn, who was a giant of a man with a big, deep voice. He threw me in between the sticks, and I absolutely loved it.

Soccer pitches are obviously a lot shorter, and you played with a lighter ball so I could usually kick it the full length of the field from my kick-outs and we got a lot of goals from them.

But it still took me a few games to get up to the rhythm of being a 'keeper in a different code, because switching isn't as simple as you might think. You had to be on your toes at the edge of the box and it involved much more ball control with my feet – but I loved how easy it was to win a free. You could just come for a corner and fall over, and the referee would blow his whistle.

In gaelic football, you didn't get one unless your head was nearly kicked off!

The soccer was great craic and I just loved the fun of it all. There was never any pressure. Lads would turn up after having a few pints the night before, and sometimes I could smell the beer.

We had a game one weekend against Longford Wanderers, and Robbie Stokes was playing for them. I knew him from five-a-side games around the place. He was small, but a very good striker.

A cross came in and he took flight for a bicycle kick. He connected with it sweetly, and it was heading straight for the top corner! At this stage, I had taken flight too… and produced an unmerciful save. But in the midst of my acrobatics, I collided with the post.

I was out for the count for a few seconds.

Mick ran on to see if I was okay.

'Are you alright Martin?'

'I'm sound!'

'Are you able to play on? How many fingers am I holding up?'

'Three!' says I.

That's all I can remember. I had a ring on my finger, and after the game I asked the lads where it came from? I was promptly told that it was a gift from my other half, but I frantically protested that no such lady existed. I was concussed for the entire second-half of the match… and was left still wondering about this mystery lady was who had gifted me the ring.

The lads said I was making saves I never made before, and any time the ball rolled to me I let out a little scream before picking it up and kicking it out. I still have a small scar on the side of my jaw to show for it.

There were no concussion protocols then, that's for sure. Lads often clashed heads, and would throw on a bandage and play away. Health and safety was out the door.

I played with Dynamo for two or three more years after that, and then I got involved with Longford Town's 'C' team.

Mark Devlin, Leo Devlin and Pat Hackett were all involved – legends of Longford Town and they had wanted me to join them in the winter of 1991.

I played with Mullingar Town as well against quality teams in the Leinster Senior League. It was just one step away from League of Ireland football.

We played at Dalton Park in Mullingar, and the pitch was like a snooker table. It was all an experience away from GAA and I took my time when it came to going back with Aughnasheelin.

I only went back for a few games, because I just didn't have the interest to play after the amount of effort that went in with PJ and that run with Leitrim. I had never trained as much in my life, and my interest waned for a while because soccer was such a breath of fresh air.

But I soon got that interest back when I got a letter from the Leitrim County board asking me to go in and train with the Leitrim seniors on a Saturday evening at St Felim's in Ballinamore ahead of the 1993/1994 season.

IT WAS A new year and a new chapter with Leitrim.

I had come from the under-16s and minors and going nowhere, to actually achieving something with the under-21s… before taking the break.

But I had to take this chance, because who knew what could happen. Representing your county is one of the biggest honours you can have and there was so much potential there after our under-21 success.

It took me right back to 1982, watching Martin Furlong's heroics for Offaly in that All-Ireland final. This was my chance.

PJ HAD BEEN and gone, and John O'Mahony was in his second season as manager, along with Ollie Honeyman and Joe Reynolds, who knew me from club football.

The team had beaten Galway the year beforehand, but they did everything but score against Gay Sheerin and Roscommon in the Connacht semi-final and lost 1-12 to 1-10.

Leitrim always seemed to concede silly goals at senior level and end up losing big games, but there was something brewing. Johno didn't know me personally and we had never met, but I was told years later that as soon as he came in, he wanted me on board.

He must have seen me somewhere, or heard reports from the under-21 run when we had beaten his native Mayo. Anyway, I arrived and met the players. Thomas Quinn was first-choice keeper and Martin Prior was No 2, and both of them were from Aughawillan – a senior club.

It was me against them – and I didn't know them at all.

I remember early on in the first session, we were doing a bit of messing on the training field, and Thomas and Martin decided to take a few shots on me to test me out.

We started a drill where you face away from the kicker and when the 'call' came you had to turn and try to save the shot.

But they would kick the ball a split second before the 'call', so when I turned I hadn't a hope of saving a shot… or the ball would even hit me before I knew anything about it.

They were making a fool of me and trying to rattle me. They probably saw me as this young lad who never played senior football, but I let them at it and didn't let it get to me. In hindsight, they saw me as a threat and rightly so.

But Johno was the boss, and whatever he said went. We did a few laps and runs that night to loosen the legs and get to grips with things, and get to know each other, but it was down to business from there.

If I thought PJ's training was hard, think again. We trained in Kells to allow the lads based in Dublin and at home to meet halfway so we could all do it together as one.

They had a decent set-up there at Naomh Colmcille with good lights, and we ran lap after lap of the place with no arguments at all.

We had a few challenge games in between, and back then you played three league games before Christmas and four more in the new year, before the championship began in the summer.

I was aiming to play in the first league game against Fermanagh at Brewster Park in Enniskillen. We trained hard, and I just kept my head down and minded my own business just like I did before with PJ and the under-21s.

JOHNO ALWAYS NAMED the team on a Friday night, and I was sitting in the corner of the dressing-room with the Fermanagh game less than 48 hours away.

I had the work done; it was me against Thomas and Martin. I didn't drink or smoke, had age on my side and when the hard yards had to go in, I only improved.

Johno spoke about the game and then started naming the team.

'In goals, Martin McHugh...

I said to myself, *I've made it.* All my hard work had paid off, I was No 1 in Leitrim and it would stay that way. The relief was huge, and I sat there delighted with myself and no longer had his attention as he named out the other 14 starters for the game.

It was a very proud moment for myself and my club as well, because I was only 5 feet 7 inches, and Aughnasheelin played in Division 2. This was the big leagues, and I would be *starting*.

After that, I always made a point of standing in the back row for any team photo and never knelt at the front. It was a confidence thing.

I knew I was small standing beside the rest of these big men, but I knew I was the best goalkeeper in the county, and deserved to be there.

I remember arriving at the ground and going out before everyone else to do my own warm-up. I heard the PA announcing the Leitrim team, and I could hear the cheers when my name was called out for my senior debut. My father was there too, which was brilliant. People were just happy to hear I was in, and the consensus was that we now had a decent young goalkeeper who already had championship pedigree.

We beat Fermanagh and I made a few saves to keep us in it. Every game from there, we progressed well as Johno groomed us into a team who would go places. He was very strict, but very fair. In every game or training session if he found something wrong somewhere, he always said it in a certain way.

We called it 'The Sandwich!'

He would mention something you did right, point out what you did wrong and praise you again to finish. He would never leave you hanging or on a sour note.

With PJ, if you made a mistake you knew about it during the game, you knew about it at half-time… and again after the match in front of everyone. It was just a different approach, and his method worked too.

But John O'Mahony just had everything to a higher standard again. Everything had to be done to perfection, and if you were doing laps they had to be done within a certain amount of time or you had to do more without any fuss.

If you were late for training, you had to do extra sprints. One night, we had training in Kells and I was working in the factory, and it was pelting down snow out of the heavens. It was sticking too, so I was looking forward to having the night off and was fully sure I wouldn't be forced to drive from Rooskey to north Meath in that weather.

I rang Johno and told him the snow was bad, but he insisted training was to go ahead.

He always picked me up in Longford… and this time he said he would collect me 45 minutes or an hour earlier than planned to make sure we'd arrive on time.

Every man made it to training, even if a few of the lads nearly crashed on the way there. Johno gathered us around and said, 'Lads, it's nights like this you'll remember when you win the Connacht title'.

Every player had made it, so it proved to him and us that we had something to aim for at the end of the year. On a night when so many of us could have made excuses and not turned up, there weren't any!

So, we started off with a game in the snow, and soon enough lads started acting the b*****ks throwing snowballs.

Johno's thinking was we could have a bit of fun before we got serious, and then we had around 20 minutes of carnage running after a football that we could barely see in the snow.

Ollie Honeyman put the cones out in the four corners of the field for the laps; cutting corners was the ultimate crime, and the footprints would give it away if we did.

Johno walked around the four corners to inspect our work when we were finished to see if anyone took any shortcuts. He arrived at the far corner and found evidence of footprints inside the cone.

'If you cut corners here, you'll cut them in a game!' We had to do extra sprints as a result, and learned that if one man made a mistake everyone paid for it. To this day I know who cut those corners, but I'm not going to hang them out to dry at this stage.

Everyone was blaming each other, and I was a prime suspect too because of my short legs. But it was a good session, and we definitely became a bit tougher mentally that night.

WE HAD A good league campaign and won four matches. We travelled south to play Cork, and stayed down there the night before on the banks of the Lee.

We had a light session on the morning of the match to warm-up, and Ollie Honeyman insisted that he knew Cork city well so he would guide the bus driver to the game.

We headed down towards Páirc Uí Chaoimh, but Ollie totally lost his bearings and sent us the wrong way. We were going along by the river and we could see the stands at the ground but had no idea how to get there.

As we got closer there was a barrier across the road, so we parked up and had to walk a mile or so to get to the ground. Johno being *Johno*, he made us run, and joked that it would be an extra warm-up for us before the game!

As we got closer to the field, we started bumping into supporters as we ran with our gear to get into the dressing-room and, at that stage, we just wanted to get the game out of the way because we knew we'd be up against it as it was.

Typically, we lost by a point but a huge crowd had travelled down from Leitrim. We had a massive following, and for our games in Carrick especially massive numbers were there well before throw-in.

We had won nothing, but Leitrim people knew something was stirring under O'Mahony – and our under-21 win, along with the 1993 championship victory over Galway, had conjured up a new-found hope in the county.

Our last league game was against who else, but Roscommon, and we were ahead by two points coming towards the end of it.

They had a free on the edge of the '21', and every man in green and gold was on the goal-line. The ball ricocheted off me and went over the bar for a point, but we had beaten them. It gave us serious momentum heading into the summer, and I knew the Rossies would be looking for revenge because we had relegated them in that last league game too, which made it a bit sweeter.

We had improved with every game and were silently building a serious momentum, and that was key.

Now, training for the championship was *here* and it was time to really roll up the sleeves. One Saturday morning, we gathered at the rugby club in Carrick and it lashed rain for hours. We couldn't see a blade of grass because there was that much water on the pitch, and Johno decided we'd have a game of soccer in the middle of all the puddles.

The likes of Jason Ward, Paul Kiernan and Conor McGlynn were flying in with the sliding tackles and we were covered head to toe in water and muck before the hard running had even started!

Then the whistle went to regroup, and that was our signal that the s**t was really going to hit the fan. We were told we were doing a 20-minute race… and that sounded grand because we all had good stamina.

It was usually myself, Noel Moran, Fergal Reynolds and sometimes Seamus Quinn near the front. We were all doing okay in the first five or 10 minutes, and more time passed before lads started drifting off.

With about five minutes to go there was only myself and Noel left, and I had it in my head that I *had* to beat him. The man would have given Sonia O'Sullivan a run for her money, with his big long legs and strides twice as long as mine.

But I stuck with him, and with a minute to go Johno blew his whistle again. 'Right lads, push it!'

With the line within sight and around 100 metres away, he left me for dust.

I stuck with him as best I could, but just couldn't keep up. I fell to my knees, and my breakfast came back up from my stomach and onto that flooded field. Johno gleefully told me I had just passed through the pain barrier, and it made me realise I was doing something right in his eyes despite the fact I was about to collapse.

I was pushing myself to the limit, and even though I was a goalkeeper, we all fought as one.

We still had no proper goalkeeper coaching that time, so anything the lads had to do, I had to do it too just as it was with PJ and all of the other underage

Leitrim teams. All of the other counties and clubs at that time were no different.

If I wanted lads to take shots on me or work on my kick-out, it had to be done before or after training started – and Ollie or Joe would usually do that with me.

Doing all of that training with the lads obviously helped my fitness, but it really helped my mental strength too. Johno was a big man for not telling us what he was doing or what his plans were, and that element of surprise kept us all on our toes and ensured nothing ever went stale.

For that pre-championship training we got in a sports psychologist called Bill Cogan, who would later work with Johno in Mayo too.

We'd never heard of this before – this was 1994!

CDs hadn't even taken off and here was John O'Mahony bringing in someone to really maximise our performance.

This was totally unheard of, but another example of O'Mahony going the extra mile to ensure we got the very best out of ourselves as a group. As far as we were concerned, we went and kicked a football and played games. Johno did this to help us individually and as a team so we could eventually reach our goal and become winners.

WE WENT TO a meeting one night in a hotel and after dinner there was a big chart in the corner, and 10 tables were set up for four or five players to sit at each one.

All of the tables had sheets of blank paper and pens, and we had a question to answer... *What makes us winners?*

Every table had to come up with one person to answer on behalf of the players there, and I was nominated for the job in our group.

Doing that made me more confident in myself to speak my mind. Before that, I was usually shy when it came to standing up and talking before games or in the dressing-room, even though I was always the opposite out on the field.

I would never question anything when it came to a manager or teammate, but Bill got us talking and it made us all speak our minds about what made us winners, and all sorts of angles and ideas filtered through the room.

Bill had a really strong Scottish accent, and he came over to me one day when I was practicing kick-outs.

He asked me how I felt and, a bit sceptical, I said I felt great. He asked me how my kick-outs were, and still trying to figure out what he was getting at, I said they were going nice and long.

He asked me what I was thinking about when I was kicking the ball out, and I plainly said I hoped one of our players won the ball.

He suggested changing things a small bit. He told me I had that power in the legs, but I could use it better with visualisation, a concept that was completely alien to me. He told me it was time to visualise what was going to happen *before* I actually kicked the ball. I was wondering what planet he was on.

He wasn't even a goalkeeper, and here he was telling me what to do! But I went with the flow, and planted the ball down to give it a try.

Pat Donoghue was around 60 yards away in the middle of the field, so before I lined up my kick I visualised him receiving the ball perfectly… and it worked! First time.

I put the ball down and banged it straight out to him, and it landed beautifully into his chest.

I asked Pat to head over by the sideline so I could try it again, even though it was a small bit out of my range. I visualised him getting the ball perfectly, and sure enough, flawlessly, it went straight into his chest again.

I kept using that technique the whole way through my career, and it became vital to me as a goalkeeper. That moment made me that little bit better again, even though I initially thought Bill was speaking waffle.

WE HAD TWO weeks off for Christmas in 1993, but Johno expected us to keep working away by ourselves throughout the festivities, and go easy on the chocolates and biscuit tins.

When we came back in the new year, there wasn't a ball to be seen. Lap after lap was back on the menu, with a lot of work on our speed.

We'd start off doing short sprints to each line on the field – starting with the 13-metre line and right up to the '65' and so on.

Lough Key Forest Park was the venue for training one evening, down by the lake on the outskirts of Boyle in county Roscommon. We met up at the bottom of the tower hill, and all we could see were two cones in the distance – the first one was 100 yards away, and the second one was 200 yards away. We had to run to the first cone, on to the second one and then off around by the bushes and the trees.

Johno kept talking and *talking*, and I was wondering when he was going to tell us where the finish line was.

One lap alone took us nearly 20 minutes, going around the whole area of the park. It was really tough going, but nice to do it away from a pitch for a change. We all did it, and I actually finished one of my laps ahead of Noel Moran, so I was delighted with myself, because Noel was so quick and fit.

Then Johno laid out five cones at the top of the tower hill, and we had to sprint up to them. Again, he made us train beyond what our bodies could do. We still say it now whenever we see each other – Johno ran us to within an inch of our lives.

But he carved out a mental toughness in us, and that's why we never gave up. There weren't too many training sessions we did where anyone dropped out and that collective mentality was unbreakable.

Nobody ever threw in the towel, and there were no excuses. You just did not give up when Johno was in charge. Nobody even dared to try it.

Johno continued to use his 'sandwich' method if he was trying to point out mistakes, but he singled me out one night in front of everyone for all the right reasons.

He used me as an example in front of the group about putting in the extra work to improve my kick-outs and shot-stopping for the overall benefit of the team.

He also pointed out how I was never late – probably all thanks to that old stopped clock in our kitchen many years beforehand which saw me miss the start of a match and swear I would never let it happen again.

I was always the first one on the field, and in Johno's eyes I was pushing myself to be the best regardless of whoever else was challenging me for that No 1 jersey.

Whatever about positions on the rest of the field, you were never safe as goalkeeper and I had two men snarling behind me ready for me to make a mess of things so they could take my spot.

AS THE CHAMPIONSHIP approached, we trained on Saturdays and Sundays in Páirc Sean MacDiarmada in Carrick. As usual, I would always arrive early for training and do my normal routine, but the pitch there wasn't great.

I would make my usual makeshift kicking tees, and could have 10 or 15 of them on the go over the course of an hour. By the end of the session, the ground would be so dug up you would think I was trying to set spuds on the home of

Leitrim football. George O'Toole, God rest him, was the groundsman, and he hated me arriving at the pitch. 'Get that hoor off the field!' he would roar, as I went through my usual ritual and destroyed his beloved sod.

He had to fix it all up again after I was finished, and he really had his work cut out for him!

We also had a few sessions at the wonderful Strandhill beach in Sligo. Johno always had the schedule done up three or four weeks in advance.

We had the odd night away too, which was great. We went to the Carrickdale Hotel over in Louth, right on the border just north of Dundalk.

We played Down in a challenge game in Newry, but a few of the lads went overboard afterwards on the Saturday night, as they tended to do! But we had great unity wherever we went, and that was all Johno's doing.

He made us the team we'd become later that summer.

You'd see Kells, Carrick and Forest Park all listed in the calendar... and the inclusion of Strandhill always created a lot of excitement.

We were all set for a day at the beach, but there would be no buckets and spades.

We arrived giddy with anticipation and the tide was out. But it wasn't the beach Johno was training us on – it was the sand dunes. Ollie was up on top of the dunes waiting for us, with his f***ing cones.

We didn't know whether to laugh or cry as our excitement turned to sheer dread.

There was a path up to where he was, and when we got to the top there was a massive valley down the opposite side of the dune.

We had no idea what was ahead of us. Johno told us our stamina, strength, mental toughness and character was all about to be seriously tested, and he wasn't wrong there.

He wanted us to go up and down the dunes, through the valley... back up the dunes again and back to the start. And that was just one lap.

When you are running in sand, you could take 10 steps and maybe move only two yards. Some smart-arse would always sit back and let the leaders go ahead so they could follow the footprints to make their own pathway through the slog a little bit easier.

It's not half as hard to break through the sand when someone else has already done it, but Johno copped on to that after just one lap. 'Pass that f***er out! Stop waiting for the footprints!'

But straight after that, you had lads passing each other out as we went up and down… and up and down again, like yoyos on those dreaded dunes. As tough as it was, nobody dared to give out – even when we had to do 10 more sprints up the dunes after those long and torturous laps.

And even though it was so difficult, it was great craic and it was something different again, and we would always take the mickey out of whoever broke the line.

I saw lads get sick in Strandhill who never got sick before, unless they'd had one too many the night before. But it would all stand to us, because whatever came in front of us on a match day, we'd get over it. Roscommon, Galway and Mayo would all find that out come the summer, even if they didn't expect it.

It was a huge test of our mental stamina, as Johno had promised, and we really had to push ourselves to get through it.

JOHNO WAS ALWAYS stressing that if we wanted a Connacht title, we had to do it the hard way. And we listened because he knew how to win them.

He had led his native Mayo to back-to-back Connacht crowns in 1989. He would go on to win the Nestor Cup with three different counties, but his record had already spoken for itself in early 1994.

Bill was still always there to drive us on too in his thick Scottish twang. 'Why do we doubt ourselves!? There are 32 teams playing for this championship! After one round of games, only 16 are left!'

This man, who we never knew existed, instilled a confidence and belief in us like never before. Nearly every session we had with him, he told us time and time again that we were winners and we were going to prove it.

PJ Carroll had brought the entire set-up to a different level when he arrived in 1989, and Johno was taking it all further again in year two of his reign. We had Roscommon away at Dr Hyde Park on June 5 in the quarter-final draw, and the reward for beating them would be a home match against Galway.

With all due respect, The Tribesmen were always going to beat London in their quarter-final but they were without a Nestor Cup since 1987, which was a real drought for them at this stage.

Mayo were on the other side of the draw, and had a bye to the semi-finals along with Sligo.

I was working away in the factory with my teammates Seamus Quinn and Pauric McLaughlin, and the craic at work started building a week before the game. The Rossies in the factory were always getting on our backs, saying how much we were going to lose by and all that, but we silently let them have their say without giving too much back.

We weren't cocky, but quietly confident.

At the last training session in Kells before the game, I still wasn't sure if I had done enough to keep that jersey off Martin Prior and Thomas Quinn. I still had the craic when I could, but overall I kept my head down and worked hard.

Johno, Ollie and Joe said their bits and pieces in the dressing-room, and then it was time to name the team that would play at the Hyde.

'In goals, Martin McHugh...'

I was bursting with excitement in the corner again, telling myself that I'd made it. My dream of playing senior championship football... and going back to 1982 and Martin Furlong all over again... it had come true.

I was jumping with joy inside, but I had to keep it under control. I was so elated when I got home... I was still walking on air.

But I quickly had to concentrate on beating those Rossies. I made sure I had my gear ready 24 hours beforehand, and we had been given new togs and socks for the occasion. I was a 'divil' for having different boots and studs ready for different conditions. I had two pairs of gloves, spare t-shirts... the lot, just in case.

I would always double check my gear in the morning in a panic, even though I had packed it to perfection the night before.

Whenever Johno saw lads start to get weak or doubting themselves at training, he would shout.

'Take it out on Roscommon lads!

'Take it out on Galway!

'Take it out on Mayo!

'Be thinking about these teams we are going to meet, and we'll beat the f***ers!'

He said it so many times, the words just stuck in our heads. We were training for a cause. Days like the snow in Kells, the Forest Park... and Strandhill would make us winners, just like Bill said we were.

« CHAPTER 5 »

I was caught
In the middle of a railroad track
I looked round
And I knew there was no turning back...
–'Thunderstruck' (AC/DC)

IT HAD BEEN 27 long years since Leitrim had beaten Roscommon in championship football and it was up to us to change that.

We met up at the back of the Bush Hotel in Carrick, and off we went on a bus to a secret destination to get away from the crowds and the public eye – another one of Johno's master plans he hadn't told any of us about.

There would be no distractions from the prying eyes of the public as we prepared for the game that we had done all this training for.

The back door in championship football didn't become a thing until 2001, so if we lost, our season was over. And we'd have all summer to think about it.

All those months of blood, sweat and tears would be wasted if we didn't take this chance and move on to the next stage. We drove past Dr Hyde Park in Roscommon a good three hours before the game and crowds were already starting to gather, and the excitement was building.

This was championship... and you could sense this was going to be big.

Then it started to rain, and I thought... *f**k it, I'll have to change those studs again!* I went over what gear I would wear time after time in my head.

WE GOT TO our secret destination, which was a fine guest-house a couple of miles outside the town.

There were sandwiches, soup, water and fruit, but I was never one for eating before a game. I had my breakfast and something very light, and that was it. My digestive system is so slow, that I could have breakfast today and I'd be alright until tomorrow without getting hungry at all.

We were able to walk around, kick around a football and just chat and relax. Johno, Ollie and Joe all spoke to the group and I sat there in silent concentration with the rest of the lads. There was a bit of banter going on with the boys as we killed the time until throw-in, but I was just so focused that entire day – even though the sun came out and it was time for another stud change!

I must have changed them three or four times; I'm such a freak like that.

Next thing, a squad car arrived with two Garda bikes, and I presumed one of us was in trouble but they were there to escort us to the ground. This was a new one for a Leitrim team, to say the least.

Again, Johno said nothing. Everything was always 'hush hush' with him, but we felt like royalty. He always did this, and always wanted us to be recognised. We weren't going to be any old team turning up an hour before a game at any pitch. He wanted us to feel like a winning team who were treated with respect.

It sent out a message that we were going to show people what we were made of. It was McGowan's bus, and Johno had arranged for a large printed sign to be placed in the front window… LEITRIM 1994.

We hopped on the bus to the flashing blue lights and the roar of the sirens, and that's when the nerves really kicked in.

In all my days playing football, I had never experienced anything like this before. I'm sure the Dublin, Kerry or Cork players did, but not us.

There was a surreal sense to it, even though we only had a short spin up to the pitch. But as the nerves were building and Johno stuck on a Tina Turner tape and we all listened to *Simply the Best*.

That was him all over. He did all he could to get us prepared on and off the field, and Tina was singing away as the sweats poured out of us along with a few nervy notes. But once we arrived and got into the dressing-room, I calmed down and regained my composure and focus after the few jitters on the bus.

We had just over an hour to go before throw-in, and this was it.

We went out to warm-up as a group, and just as it was in training, I went through the whole regime with the rest of the team.

When we jogged towards the sideline we could hear our supporters egging us on as they made their way inside. And I could hear the odd roar of… 'C'MON McHUGH!' as well.

It was hard to keep your mind tuned in with all of this going on, but it was very exciting too. My senior championship debut was upon me.

My hard work had paid off, and as we made our way back inside thousands were still pouring into the ground. Johno said his final bits and pieces, and when we ran out to the field again we were greeted by an enormous cheer.

It was a remarkable reception to get from our own inside the lion's den.

We could sense in the air that something major was going to happen, as we stood for a team photo and got another warm-up going at the graveyard end goal, where a lot of our supporters were.

Even though this was championship, everyone could still hear me roaring like a lunatic through the entire match once the ball was thrown in.

I WAS SHOUTING at my backs to keep them on their toes, and tried to keep my own focus too as a really tight game started to play out.

It was really nip and tuck the whole way through, even though everything our forwards kicked seemed to go over the bar. George Dugdale got a crucial goal for us after just 13 minutes to end a brilliant team move.

George was a real playmaker and a huge talent. He was really fit, focused and so determined every time he got the ball. A goal or a point was always on his mind once he got a hold of it. He was an incredible athlete.

But in previous years when Leitrim played Roscommon, the Rossies always seemed to get a goal just before half-time. Deep into stoppage time at the end of the first-half, a high ball came in. Seamus Quinn jumped for it, but it broke to Don Connellan and he took a rasper of a shot.

It was a glorious chance for a goal.

Somehow, I saved it with my left knee and turned it around the post for a '45' to deny him.

Had he scored, who knows?

We went in 1-8 to 0-5 in front at the break. It was a commanding lead, but there was a long way to go.

Johno kept us calm at the break and focused on the positives. He complimented my kick-outs as I sat there in silence, mentally preparing myself for standing in the town end goal for the next 35 minutes with the Roscommon supporters at my back.

It was jammed full of Rossies down there, and they never stopped.

'PUT ON YOUR F***ING WELLIES MCHUGH!

'LOOK AT THE SIZE OF YA McHUGH! YOU'RE TWO FOOT NOTHIN!'

'YA LITTLE WIMP!'

Thankfully, I didn't have too much to do in the second-half, and my backs were really on their toes. They had little choice with me barking at them either!

We only scored two points in that second-half, but we held on to win by the minimum – 1-10 to 0-12. Aiden Rooney scored five points, and George's goal was just vital. Liam Conlon got two important points as well, and Colin McGlynn had a big game at full-forward even though he didn't score.

Derek Duggan got six points for them, and a nippy little corner-forward by the name of Shane Curran – who would become an iconic goalkeeper for the county and St Brigid's – was held scoreless.

He did get on the end of a brilliant goal chance but his shot was superbly blocked by Joe Honeyman and we frantically cleared. Shane created a lot of trouble for us even though he didn't score himself.

The Rossies kept coming at us and won the second-half 0-7 to 0-2. Duggan had a glorious chance to level it with the last kick of the game from a free from around 50 metres out, but he went for power and drove it wide.

And crucially, Roscommon kicked 15 wides that day which meant our first-half surge was enough to win the game… just about.

Wexford referee Brian White blew for full-time… and, instantly, so much emotion poured out from us and our supporters as wild scenes unfolded.

We knew at the start of the year that we would have to beat all three… Roscommon, Galway and Mayo to win that Connacht title, and we were over the first hurdle.

Everyone in Leitrim had waited a long time for this… a lot of us weren't even born the last time it happened. When you are so focused on a game for so long, it's just all released when that whistle blows. We could finally relax… and celebrate.

There were hundreds of Leitrim people running onto the pitch, jumping wires and fences to come on and bask in the glory of it all and celebrate with us. It took us an age to get back to the dressing-room, between meeting people and family members, and I met my father out on the field too which was a lovely moment. Everyone was so happy and proud… it meant the world.

Next thing, supporters were asking us for autographs. *Autographs,* imagine! I had never signed an autograph in my life.

This was just the first round of the championship, but it just added to the sense of achievement. We could have easily got caught up in all of that but, thankfully, we didn't. We knew this was *only* step one. But we had to enjoy the moment too.

I signed footballs, jerseys, match programmes and *whatever else.* A Roscommon reporter, Seamus Duke was there and he asked me what it was like to beat the Rossies on their home patch?

I said it was great, that a lot of hard work went in and all of that stuff. But my father was actually originally from Slatta in Roscommon, and didn't Seamus ask me if there was any truth that I should have been playing for them instead.

My reply was, 'F**k no! I'm a Leitrim man through and through!'

But that was the end of the conversation, because we were live on the radio and I had just sworn on air in the middle of the day on a Sunday. Seamus probably had to apologise to his listeners.

But the celebrations went on and on, and the dressing-room was absolutely buzzing when we eventually got back into it. In fairness to him, Johno was quick to shift our minds to the next task. He wanted us to enjoy the night, but we had more work to do and we had training again on Tuesday night.

We got back on the bus and headed for Carrick to have dinner, and the hotel was jammed with supporters. You'd swear we had won *something,* but that ambition never got lost in the madness.

I WAS LIVING in Newtownforbes in Longford at the time. My second child, Emma, had been born in April so I couldn't stay out too late, but I still had time to pop into Cox's pub in Dromod on my way home.

I regularly called in when I was passing, and was hardly going to pass now after our famous victory. I landed in and they were all about me, asking how it felt to beat Roscommon? And all the craic and banter started as I had my soft drinks and a few laughs, and the lads downed their pints in party mode.

They kept mentioning the save I made to deny Connellan just before half-time, so personally it was nice to hear that I was doing my bit to help the cause as they all patted me on the back with sheer delight.

I was off work on the Monday, but I strolled into that factory on the Tuesday morning with my head held high I can tell you.

We'd been listening to it all week at work before the match in that factory. It was the Leitrim workers against the Roscommon workers when it came to everything in there, so beating them made it extra sweet.

The Rossies had been flat out reminding us how they beat us the previous year in the championship, and I was flat out playing the card that we had sent them packing down to Division 3.

But this week, there wasn't a word from them.

They were like mice and there wasn't a peep from them, but we kept the slagging going and we enjoyed the moment for days. We went back training that Tuesday night and everyone was still on a serious high… but there were four cones dotted around the field waiting to take us back down to earth with very few footballs in sight.

JOHNO CALLED US into a huddle, and the s**t was about to hit the fan all over again. As seismic as it was, beating the Rossies had to be parked as it was only the first step on our journey.

He re-emphasised the great work we had done and the result, but it was time to move on and get the heads down all over again to focus on beating Galway. It was back to laps upon laps… and they were all timed. We would run four laps, three laps, two… and then one – followed by the same in reverse, so you clocked up at least 18 of them.

It was really tough, intense training but it had to be done to give us all a reality check and flush the victory, and the celebrations that followed, out of our systems.

We were run within an inch of our lives again that night in Kells, and half of the panel must have thrown up at some stage! We went again on Friday night in Carrick and it was more hard running but, thankfully, with a bit more ball work.

But, given the four-week gap between matches, we found ourselves back in Strandhill on the Saturday… and there was no rest for the wicked.

It was a really warm evening, and the sand was bone dry with no grip in it at all. You could go around 40 steps and only gain two yards.

A normal run on the hill would take five minutes, but that evening it took double that because the sand was just pulling the legs off us. It was hard going like that for two weeks, but Johno always did it in a way that the runs eventually got shorter and shorter, and our stamina remained high.

One night we had to do 10 x 45-metre runs, and everyone did it because our fitness and stamina was through the roof – including my own. But as it always was, any time I wanted to do something in terms of my goalkeeping I still had to do it before or after the main session. I must have been the fittest goalkeeper in the country that year.

We had in-house games and played one or two challenge matches as well to keep us match-sharp. And, before we knew, it was championship week again. Galway were on the horizon.

It was the same routine as it was for the Roscommon match… and we trained on the Tuesday and Friday before the game.

Johno named the team and it was more or less the same 15. I was delighted to keep my place. I still had to do the work to keep the jersey, and treat every session like it was my last. If we had to do runs, I wanted to finish first or second and it was the same if we were doing sprints. If we were playing a game, I knew if I made a mistake all eyes would be on me and I could be dropped like a hot plate.

From my viewpoint it wouldn't take much for lads to say I wasn't up to it, because I was on the short side and I came from a club that didn't play senior football. Those factors were constantly working against me all the time. That's why keeping my place always came with a bit of relief.

I kept raising the bar no matter what, because I knew if I dropped things a notch I'd be cut from the team. So, whatever had to be done, I did it to the best of my ability every single time. That had me ready for Galway and whatever they were going to throw at us.

THIS TIME WE were at home in Carrick.

Johno had already won two Connacht titles with Mayo, and knew what it took to beat the men in maroon. They must have been sick of the sight of him, until of course, he went there himself and won them two Sam Maguires.

The likes of Kevin Walsh from Killannin and Tuam's Ja Fallon were emerging for them and they had some really classy players, just like Galway always did.

Again, they hadn't won the Nestor Cup since 1987 so they were eager to end their own famine. Seven years was a long time for Galway to go without a Connacht title... and Mayo man O'Mahony on the line for us really added spice to the occasion.

We had a man in our ranks called Peter Harvey, who would always scope out the opposition for us. He was like our very own spy, and a serious character. He would do whatever it took to get what he wanted, and even used to ask for videos of games off other teams and make up some silly story that someone in America wanted to see it in order to get the footage. I was briefed to keep my kick-outs away from big Walsh in the middle of the field. Of course, Kevin became an astute coach himself and managed Sligo before getting the Galway job and winning two Connacht titles with them as the man in charge.

Mickey Quinn was going to be marking Walsh and was told to drag him out to the sideline on the stand side of the field in Carrick, and do whatever it took to minimise his influence on the game.

If Kevin didn't follow him, Mickey would be free but I still had to drive the ball as long as I could and trust my players to fight for it and win it after that.

Fallon and Niall Finnegan were real dangermen for Galway, and our half-forwards were well warned about Sean Óg de Paor – the attacking half-back who was extremely dangerous and would also prove that on the biggest stage later in his career.

He was just a wonderful footballer and he went on to win two All Star awards.

When Johno was briefing the lads out the field on their opponents and jobs, I was barely listening because I was just so wrapped up in myself and my own task to keep the Galway forwards at bay... and keep the ball out of my net again.

Every game was the same for me in that regard, deciding quickly where my kick-outs would go, and just keeping my mind concentrated on everything I had to do... from barking at my defenders... having the right studs... keeping clean-sheets.

WE MET UP at the Bush Hotel again before the game, and off we went to another mystery bed and breakfast a few miles outside the town. I had no idea it even existed, but again Johno had it all organised.

It was up a really narrow road beside a little lake, and again there was tea, sandwiches and fruit, all laid out for us so we could just chill out before the big one.

Johno said nothing as usual, but it was the same idea as before the Roscommon game just to help us relax and keep us cocooned away from the crowd, because over 10,000 were expected at the game.

We had a bit of a chat, and lo and behold the squad car and two Garda motorbikes arrived again to guide us through the thronging town and escort us to Páirc Sean, because this year Leitrim meant business.

The tunes were blaring away on the bus, but often when I heard music before a match the damn song would be in my head in the warm-up… and stick around until the first ball arrived in the game!

But Tina Turner had been silenced.

Thunderstruck by AC/DC blared through the bus, and Angus Young's guitar riffs boomed through the speakers. It wasn't the worst tune to have stuck inside your head before a game, because it really got me going and there were no nerves this time.

We were driving up towards the ground and for a good half a mile before we got there, all you could see were the Leitrim supporters and the flags and the banners.

They were cheering like mad when they spotted us. Between that and AC/DC screaming through the bus, we were seriously revved up. The dressing-rooms in Carrick were a bit tighter than they are now, but we togged out and got our minds in gear again. We ran out to warm-up, and again I could hear my name being shouted from the people on the terraces. Leitrim had beaten Galway the year before too, and the visitors were here for payback.

I hit a few kick-outs in the warm-up, and my confidence had grown even more because I had that championship debut against the Rossies under my belt. This was new territory no more, and I was ready.

We went back into the dressing-room and Johno gave us one last talking to, to really rev us up, and we ran back out like men possessed to an enormous cheer. We had caught the imagination of the Leitrim people, and they were really getting behind us as the ball was thrown in by Mayo referee Sean McHale.

It was another tight affair – even though we thought we had a dream start.

A long free from Declan Darcy was punched into the net by Jason Ward, but it was chalked off for a square ball. Somehow, there was no score for the first 15 minutes, and both teams were guilty of kicking poor wides. It felt like playing in a soccer match! Finally, Aiden Rooney, George Dugdale and Paul Kieran all scored for us and we led, 0-3 to 0-2 at half-time – just to sum up how poor some of the shooting was. I felt no nerves beforehand, but it was glaringly obvious that wasn't the case for some of my teammates.

You could see there was pressure on a few of the lads, and we weren't playing well at all. We were working hard, but making hard work of it in front of our own.

JUST 50 SECONDS after the restart, I was picking the ball out of my net at the town end. Conor McGauran had broken free, and buried one past me to give them the lead for the first time.

I'm always p****d off when I concede a goal, but you can't dwell on it and just have to switch your concentration to the next ball. If a goal goes in, you just have to think about not letting it happen again… park it straightaway.

But it's always nerve-racking, because it generates a huge cheer and your opponents gain all of the momentum to go with it. The buck stops with the goalkeeper in preventing that happening.

However, I still had a big job to do. The match was far from over. It was tit-for-tat for the rest of the game. George Dugdale was keeping us in it.

He kicked three points.

Aidan Rooney and Paul Kieran kicked a couple of points each too, but we were struggling overall. Somehow, we were level at 1-5 to 0-8 in stoppage time… Fergal O'Neill and Fallon had scored two points each for Galway, on top of McGauran's goal.

And when McGauran pointed in the 73rd minute, it looked like we were dead and buried.

With seconds to go, however, we had a free to rescue the game and our season when Galway defender John Fallon was found guilty of charging.

The kick was over 45 metres out, but you always trusted Darcy to produce the goods in those situations.

Of course, Declan delivered under all that pressure.

He stuck it over the bar to draw it right at the death. If there was one man you wanted to kick that ball, it was him. It was the only score he got that day, but the only one that mattered. It was, literally, the last kick of the game, and we were off the hook big time.

We had kicked 11 wides, even though Galway had 14.

Needless to say, Johno was not one bit happy in the changing-room. Steam was coming out of his ears, because we were just terrible.

He asked if it was the hard training behind the performance? He was baffled as to what happened to us. We just weren't focused. We were just so far off the mark compared to the Roscommon game a month beforehand.

THE REPLAY WAS a week later in Tuam. Nobody was allowed a drop of drink. We were sent straight home to think about what went wrong and what we had to do to fix it.

The day after the game, Ireland were playing in the knockout stages of the World Cup against Holland in Orlando.

The whole country was going mad following 'Jack's Army' that summer and the team had qualified from its group after that famous 1-0 win over Italy in New Jersey. Johno told us to watch the game at home and not go to any pubs.

I looked on in horror as Packie Bonner had a big 'off-day' and the Dutch won 2-0 to send Ireland home.

Johno had spies everywhere. I don't think too many lads broke the rules. We never questioned anything he asked us to do.

Ireland's World Cup was over, but our summer was still very much alive. We met up again on the Tuesday night in Kells, and we spent an hour and a half working with the ball and some shooting to get our minds back in the zone again.

We had to go into the lions' den for the replay!

But Leitrim had beaten Galway in Tuam the year before, for the first time in 44 years, so... at least that hoodoo was gone, but we knew we were really up against it if we were to do it all over again.

We hadn't been in a Connacht final since 1967.

We hadn't won it since 1927... our only Nestor Cup.

Johno maintained that the final was there for us if we wanted it. It was all about how prepared we were to battle until the end, and how badly we wanted to really suffer and go through the pain barrier all over again.

Bill came in again, and always got confidence out of us in the way he told us things. We had three hurdles in front of us at the start of that championship.

We were over one, struggled past the next but the same reward was still there for all of the hard work. He made us think about what had to be done, and his methods really made us believe we could do it.

JOHNO ALWAYS DROVE at us and pushed us, but he never picked out any players individually for criticism, or told anyone they were useless. He always strived to get the very best out of us every single time.

This was why we had done all of the excruciating training in Kells, Strandhill and Forest Park in the muck and the rain and the snow.

Did half of us puke our guts up, just to lose to Galway in Tuam? We had a golden opportunity to get to a Connacht final, and very few Leitrim people get that.

As Johno always said… 'Don't f**k this up!'

The onus was on us to be better every time… for every kick, every pass… and it all had to be perfect. This had all been drilled into us for months.

I STILL HAD to focus on my own little area, my patch in that goalmouth and the small square. I might have been small, but I was the best… and I had to keep telling myself that.

I still made sure I was standing in the back row of every team photo beside all the big lads like Liam Conlon, Colin McGlynn and Mickey Quinn.

The replay in Tuam was incredibly nerve-racking. We had our Garda escort again, and the streets towards St Jarlath's Park were very narrow as we made our way there flanked by throngs of supporters.

The bus was at a crawl.

We were recognising people making their way to the match, and giving them a smile and a wave.

Again, it felt like we were doing something for a very special cause.

We wanted to win for those supporters and for Leitrim people everywhere, because it felt like the whole county was behind us – to say they were crying out for success was a serious understatement.

It made me realise if we knuckled down and got through this game, something really magical could happen that would not only put us into legendary status as players, but give our people something amazing that they could hold onto forever.

JUST NINE MINUTES in, and we were two points ahead thanks to Colin

McGlynn's brilliance after just 16 seconds and a Barney Breen free... when Liam Conlon won a penalty.

But George's weak shot was saved by my opposite number Martin McNamara, which did little to help the nerves.

There wasn't even a chance from a rebound... as McNamara held onto it! And Galway were able to work the ball out the field again.

Someone was blowing a whistle on the terrace too, which added to the jitters. The referee Sean McHale even stopped play for a minute to ask whoever was at it to stop!

But again, Galway kicked wides.

Ja Fallon uncharacteristically dropped one short into my hands, and he also kicked a wide along with Feargal O'Neill. Our heads remained above water. We went in 0-5 to 0-2 in front at the break... not a bad position at all, after Barney had scored a couple of frees.

We were just so determined not to lose, and the harsh words from Johno after the drawn game were still ringing in our ears.

My job was to keep a clean-sheet and make sure my defenders were organised, and it was all clicking into place as we were miles better than the week before.

This was the real us... history beckoned.

Seamus Quinn was having a huge game in front of me, even though I never stopped shouting at him and the rest of our defenders.

Shay Walsh, De Paor, Kevin Walsh and Fallon hit unanswered scores early in the second-half to get Galway going again and, suddenly, they were one point ahead... 0-6 to 0-5. For the Kevin Walsh point, I landed a kick-out straight out to him and he obliged to split the posts. It proved just how dangerous he was and why there was so much talking about him in our dressing-room.

WE DIDN'T SCORE for the first 11 minutes of the half and, finally, George got one over the bar to end what seemed an eternity. The game was level again.

Aiden Rooney kept us in it coming down the stretch, as Galway kept coming at us and were being seriously driven on by the home crowd. But on the hour mark, Colin got the score of the game when his blistering run finished a perfect team move. Shay Walsh and Aiden Rooney swapped scores at each end, before Val Daly levelled the game heading into stoppage time.

But Padraig sent over a beauty at the other end for us with 73 minutes on the clock and the end in sight.

The huge hurdle was being jumped… as long as we held our nerve.

That stubbornness, character and refusal to be beaten had shone through again. I think I barely touched the ball in the second-half, bar from kick-outs, as the lads out the field made sure Galway never got a sniff at goal.

ALL THE SAME, the remaining minutes and seconds seemed like an eternity.

Apparently, one Leitrim woman spent the final moments on her knees, praying to the Heavens that we got over the line. Someone up there certainly listened to her.

De Paor flashed the ball wide with the last kick of the game… and it could have been curtains, because there were teammates free either side of him. But he opted to shoot himself.

Our selector Joe Reynolds was whistling and shouting from the line for the ref to blow it up! The Leitrim fans were preparing to flood the field!

After 77 long and torturous minutes, the whistle finally blew… and this time it wasn't anyone messing in the stands.

It was sheer elation as our fans streamed onto the pitch. The hurdle had been jumped… we were clear. The extra game also made us better, stronger and only filled us with more belief that we could achieve something major on the back of this seismic performance. We had beaten Roscommon, drawn with Galway and then sent them packing in their own backyard.

WE WERE ON the verge of history.

We were so close to becoming heroes.

We were 70 minutes away from it… if we wanted it after 67 long years.

The dressing-room was hopping, but it wasn't long before the mood and focus switched. There and then, Johno sat us down and brought us back down to earth and echoed what he had already told the media outside.

He had one last request… 'Show me the cup!'

PART THREE

The Road to Croker

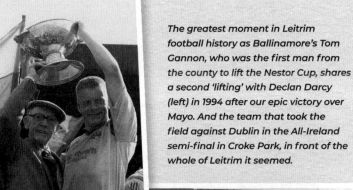

The greatest moment in Leitrim football history as Ballinamore's Tom Gannon, who was the first man from the county to lift the Nestor Cup, shares a second 'lifting' with Declan Darcy (left) in 1994 after our epic victory over Mayo. And the team that took the field against Dublin in the All-Ireland semi-final in Croke Park, in front of the whole of Leitrim it seemed.

« CHAPTER 6 »

EVERY STREET, ROAD, laneway… every nook and cranny in Leitrim had flags on it as soon as we had beaten Galway. The atmosphere around the place was just huge.

One evening, I went out to my homeplace to help my father with a bit of turf… and green and gold was everywhere to be seen in the village. There was a big banner at Aughnasheelin's pitch wishing me luck. It brought tears to my eyes. This was my own club illustrating their pride and support for me, and it meant the world.

I drove down by Ballinaglera, in the back of beyond near the border with Fermanagh, and there were flags everywhere. Every man, woman and child had been gripped by Leitrim mania. But now they needed us to deliver. If we did, we were legends forever. Others might have felt the pressure with that level of hype but, honestly, the way we had been prepared for this summer… we embraced it.

MY FAMILY WAS getting phone calls all week from people wishing me luck, and it gave a real sense of occasion when relations in England and America were ringing up my parents to pass on their best wishes. We realised we were representing Leitrim people and their friends all over the world.

We were representing our clubs, our parishes… and our county. And I was wearing No 1 for Leitrim in a Connacht final against a big, strong Mayo team.

A year before that, I was *nowhere*… I was a *nobody*, and gaelic football wasn't even on my radar. The hype didn't stay away from the work-place either. Before we played Galway, all the Rossies at the factory were in my ear again saying we were going to lose. They really wanted to see our summer ending.

I walked back into work on the Monday after the Galway replay proud as punch once more. Funnily enough, those lads at work slowly started getting behind us then. Maybe this was because it was Mayo against us in the final, and the Rossies actually wanted them to lose even more than they wanted us beaten!

THE SATURDAY AFTER the Galway victory, we went for a night away to the Slieve Russell Hotel in Cavan. Because of the replay, we only had a fortnight to prepare for the big one against Mayo at Dr Hyde Park, but the smaller gap was actually better to keep the momentum going. The McGovern brothers from Aughavas were huge supporters of Leitrim football, along with Jimmy O'Connor's pub in Dromod. Their support made a huge difference to our preparations for the game, and facilitated our night away in Cavan.

It meant a lot to be brought away to a top-class hotel, even though nobody knew what was going on! Typically, Johno had said nothing again. We had trained in Carrick that day, and it was a right good session. Johno turned to us and told us there was a bus waiting for us to go away… and nobody had a clue about it.

He wanted to get us away, so we could gather our thoughts. He also wanted us cocooned from the hype that was going into overdrive from fans and the media alike. It was actually a perfect little 'mental rest'.

It would have been very easy to get side-tracked by all of the hysteria in the county, and Johno wanted to protect us from that circus. We only had two or three more training sessions to go before the final, and each was precious.

As we all arrived in Kells for one of our final sessions before the game, I noticed all the cones and footballs were out. With the game so close, we were all ready for a nice handy evening. Johno gathered everyone in a huddle, and said that two masseurs were present to give everyone a good rub down. These were the days before big backroom teams and we didn't even have a physio – but he had two there that night to help us out with any niggles – Susan Burke and the one and only Mick Byrne!

Mick was the Irish soccer physio, and was synonymous with all of Jack Charlton's teams during that golden era for the 'Boys in Green'. He became immortalised in Irish sport before Ireland's Euro '88 tie with England in Stuttgart.

'We'll do them for yis today!' he roared up at Irish supporters as he carried gear into the changing room, and the old enemy were beaten 1-0 thanks to Ray Houghton's iconic goal. Mick had just returned from his second World Cup in America, and here he was helping Leitrim get ready for the Connacht final. We were stunned. What an honour to have him!

We all lined up to get our massages and I was up next at Mick's table, and he nearly pulled the legs off me! His hands were rough as sandpaper, rubbing and stretching every sinew and muscle I had worked on since starting out with Leitrim. We chatted for a bit, and I told him who I was and where I played. He walked away to his kit bag and returned with a pair of black Ireland shorts that had been worn by the great Packie Bonner. I was gobsmacked!

Here I was getting a rub down from a legend just home from the World Cup, and now I have a pair of Packie Bonner's shorts that he wore in goals playing for Ireland!

It was another masterstroke from Johno, getting him in. Ireland had been synonymous with a winning mentality under Big Jack, and Mick was always a visible presence beside him on the sideline. His arrival gave us another huge psychological boost more than anything, and he showed up again here and there a few times after that.

Mick was also back in with Johno when he took the Galway job in 1998, and they remain very close friends.

Bill, of course, was there to help us get into the right frame of mind again, and ensure that we knew full well what we needed to do to become Connacht champions. He opened up a flip-board. There were three words there.

CONNACHT CHAMPIONSHIP WINNERS.

He flipped to the next page. One question.

WHY CAN THIS NOT BE ACHIEVED?

He put it back on us. We were asked what we could do individually and as a team to make it happen. The meeting went on for a good hour and a half. We all spoke. We told one another how much we wanted to win. And we reminded one another what we had to do. Bill even got me talking in front of the group, and talking with confidence. That didn't happen too often. The same applied for Fergal Reynolds and Seamus Quinn. We were all talking about what it would take to win, and what it would mean.

WE HAD BEEN hearing it constantly at training from Johno.

'70 MINUTES!

'70 MINUTES...

'HEROES FOR THE REST OF YOUR LIVES!'

We had the work done. Johno never once flinched that it was his own Mayo who stood in our way. We had been to hell and back to beat Roscommon and Galway to get here. Physically and mentally... we were... READY!

WE HAD A light session on the Friday before the game, and went to a hotel for something to eat. Then it was time to name the team. We were called into a meeting room for the last brief before the day of the game. I was confident I'd still be in the team... and I was. Ollie and Joe said a few words, and when Johno spoke... we hung on his every word.

Mayo were reigning champions, and Johno had a hold of a newspaper headline that announced... *MAYO 35, LEITRIM 1*. This was the Connacht championship roll of honour. He had managed Mayo to two of those himself, but told us... 'Change that headline lads!' That's all he had to say. He never over-emphasised things or went into overly grand detail. He would say something short and snappy like that, and put it back on us. We returned home with that headline loud in our heads, right until we lay down to go to sleep.

IRONICALLY, WE HAD to stay away from newspapers for the rest of the weekend. If anyone tried to talk to us about the match, we had to walk away or change the subject... but I did the opposite! On my way home from Carrick, I stopped off at Jimmy O'Connor's pub in Dromod for a Club Orange, which was a little ritual of mine. When I left there, I popped into the Weir Lodge in Rooskey while I was at it. A few of the lads from work were there, wishing me luck and asking me how I was feeling? I wanted to get a feel of the build-up for myself, and that was my way of doing it.

It wasn't as if I was in there sinking pints, in fairness. I wasn't fully clued in for the game yet. It was still 48 hours away. You can overthink things, and I sidelined that by letting other people talk about it and experiencing some of the build-up for myself. But on the morning of the match – July 24, 1994 – I was sh***ing blocks! The nerves were in full flow, as was everything else.

I had diarrhoea, and genuinely thought I was in big trouble. I fretted more than ever before about being late and having all of my gear ready on top of it all.

The team doctor, Dr Loftus said it was down to pure nerves, and gave me a tablet to settle things. The game was at Dr Hyde Park, which already had good memories for us. We got on the bus to Roscommon and everyone was really relaxed as we pulled up at the same guest-house just outside the town where we had visited before playing the Rossies in the quarter-finals.

My nerves were still building. We could hear foghorns and noise coming from the town as crowds started to descend on the Hyde.

Johno brought us inside for some tea and a chat, and then we went back outside. Some lads were kicking a football about just to pass the time. I didn't want to go near a ball for fear of pulling a hamstring or something like that, so I let them at it. I strolled around and checked my gear again. And finally, it was time to go. The bus was going slowly towards the ground, and a sea of Leitrim flags gradually came into view. Again, *Thunderstruck* was the music of choice to get us going. There was very little said on the bus.

Today was different. Today was unlike any other day we had ever experienced in our lives. Players nowadays have their heads down on the bus to a game, with the earphones in, but soaking up the atmosphere and listening to heavy rock music never did us any harm. The Hyde was absolutely jammed.

Every Leitrim person across the globe had bought into the hype and were behind us… and they all seemed to be there in Roscommon town. Time was ticking until throw-in… the sense of occasion was growing all the time. It was nearly time! Time to do or die… *THIS DAY!*

It all boiled down to this… and who wanted it the most. This time, the cup was here! The Nestor Cup. Leaving for home without it was unthinkable.

MAYO WERE MANAGED by Kerry legend Jack O'Shea. They were the reigning Connacht champions, even though Cork had hammered them 5-15 to 0-10 in the 1993 All-Ireland semi-final.

But O'Shea was a seven-time All-Ireland winner with Kerry, and he had fantastic players on that team like Pat Fallon and Colm McManamon, but Liam McHale was their main man. He was a colossus, and admired throughout the country as being one of Ireland's greatest sportsmen… full stop!

A young Ciarán McDonald was on the bench, and what a hero he would turn out to be later in his career. But despite all the talk about our opposition and their hot favourites tag, I tried to stay focused on us. *On my own game.*

In the dressing-room, I was in the left-hand corner. I could just never sit in the middle. I liked it in the corner, where I was kind of left alone with my own thoughts.

I could still sense the serious mood. I got up to hop the ball against the wall in the showers… to loosen out my shoulders. I felt like a caged animal. I wanted to get out. And then, it was time… TO GO! Darcy said his last few words, and we left. This was it. If there was a lock on the door, we would have busted through it because we were more than ready. A rapturous roar rang around the ground. We went onto that field at a hundred miles an hour to a deafening noise.

The hair on the back of my neck was standing up. There was over 18,000 packed into the place. It was the biggest crowd I had ever played in front of – and I was leaping and jumping, just to get my legs going. But we had to stand quietly, solemnly for the team photo. That didn't help my nerves.

I HAD WORN a white jersey against Roscommon and Galway. This time, I was in blue with a gold trim to avoid a potential clash with the Mayo goalkeeper Barry Heffernan. He wore white with a blue trim. At Johno's insistence our players wore gold. Mayo, even though they were the defending champs, had to revert to a changed red strip.

But the crest was all that mattered. All of our hard work boiled down to this final moment, as we warmed-up one last time at the graveyard end.

We felt we had every scenario covered at training… including any mistakes. Johno always emphasised that we were not to dwell on it if things went wrong!

It was, always, about the next ball, and that would prove to be the case more than ever in the game about to commence.

« CHAPTER 7 »

THE BALL WAS thrown in by Galway referee Mick Curley.

And straightaway… DISASTER!

Pat Fallon sent in a high ball for Mayo… and I called for it.

But Seamus Quinn cut across me and went for it… it went through our hands.

It landed in the back of the net.

Fifteen seconds.

'F**k it!' said Seamus.

I agreed.

SEAMUS WALKED BACK out to his position with his head down, but I gave him a good pat on the back.

I told him not to worry about it.

'Let's get them back, let's get our own goal!'

We didn't even mention it after that, and we barely spoke about it at half-time either, thank God. I launched my kick-out down the field… and it was game on again.

If you are going to let in a goal, early in the game is the best time. But we weren't settling at all… and Liam Conlon, Aiden Rooney, Fergal Reynolds and Paul Kieran all kicked wides at the other end.

We were giving the ball away cheaply too.

FINALLY, WE GOT our first score after eight minutes.

Padraig Kenny kicked a great point. At my end, Kevin Staunton hit one wide, and Kevin O'Neill hit a free against the post, before John Conmy hit the upright twice from shots at goal. Suddenly, it was Mayo missing the target and shaking a bit.

After 18 minutes, McHale was booked for a late hit on Darcy. It meant their star man had to be careful for the rest of the day.

And somehow, they didn't get any points in that whole first-half. Paul Kieran levelled the game from a free and Aiden Rooney, Mickey Quinn and Liam Conlon all scored to give us a 0-6 to 1-0 lead at the break.

Shipping that early nightmare goal was well out of our systems, and the biggest 35 minutes of our lives was ahead of us now... with a three-point lead in the bank. An hour earlier, we would have given our right arms for that scoreline at the break.

Mayo just kept missing, but our defence was rock solid too... helped, of course, by me roaring and shouting like a lunatic as usual.

Seamus Quinn, Joe Honeyman and Fergal Quinn were on their toes all the time and the same went for Noel Moran, Darcy and Gerry Flanagan in front of them. Big McHale was failing to have the impact they wanted.

We knew Mayo were very good at breaking down attacks and coming at teams quickly when they turned the ball over, so we did really well bar that first 15 seconds. But despite our lead, there was nobody getting ahead of themselves in the dressing-room. There was a sense that *something* could happen here, but we weren't there yet.

There was a long way to go.

Even though we were three points ahead and in a good position, Johno reminded us that he still didn't see any cup and this was only the halfway mark.

If we took our eye off the ball now, we'd be going home with *nothing* and would have the rest of the summer to think about it. There were harsh words for the lads who weren't performing. Then, we had to recompose ourselves.

Joe Reynolds spoke, and said that it was there for us if we wanted it. We knew we were on the edge of history and were within touching distance of being heroes forever. This was for our families, our friends, our neighbours.

For us, for Leitrim! We had a huge opportunity in front of us to etch ourselves into the history of Leitrim football forever.

We all stood up and started banging things and cheering. We ran back out on the field even faster than we did before the game.

The second-half was a tighter affair.

It took us time to settle in again. O'Shea was clearly unhappy with how things were going for Mayo, and he took Tony Morley and John Conmy off just two minutes in, with John Casey and Ronan Golding came on.

Darcy sent a free over the bar. We were up and running again, before Aiden Rooney sailed over a beauty to put us five ahead.

My kick-outs were going well.

Things were looking good.

But Mayo gave us a huge warning when McHale hit the post just five minutes in. Then I made a big save to deny Golding, when he must have been sure he had scored.

Darcy scored for us at the other end.

Mickey Quinn got a wonderful score when he fooled the Mayo defence with a sweet dummy and planted it over the bar.

There were 20 minutes left.

A high Peter Butler ball came in to my left. Colm McManamon punched it goal-wards but I was there to thwart him again, and I won a free out when I clattered against him. Colm was a big man, and all I could see was his chest in front of me when I hit the ground and rolled over. Curley blew the whistle in my favour.

Golding cut our lead back to six.

Then McDonald entered the game and pointed.

Mayo were making one last giant effort, and then… AGAIN!

DISASTER AGAIN!

With 64 minutes on the clock, they won a penalty.

A THROUGH BALL from McHale found Casey.

Our defence was all at sea. Casey was a brilliant forward from Charlestown and he side-stepped me before Joe Honeyman brought him down.

Golding stepped up to take it.

He started his run… and I waited.

WHACK!

I dived low to my left.

I saved it.

My ears were ringing with the noise from the crowd… when… REAL DISASTER!

Kevin O'Neill palmed the rebound over my head… the ball looped into the net. TOTAL DISASTER!

Suddenly, there was only a score in it.

I WAS GUTTED, and disgusted.

There's nothing worse than making a huge save like that and then being done by the rebound. I got good power behind the save, but O'Neill was just so quick to react ahead of my defenders to jump and palm it in.

There was actually confusion when he scored, because the ball bounced straight out again off the back stanchion that went across the goal to support the netting.

Some of our players and supporters thought he had missed, but the referee was a Garda Inspector… and he and his umpires were in no doubt.

The score stood, and rightly so.

0-12 to 2-3.

I was so p***ed off that I lashed the resulting kick-out over the sideline towards the stand side of the ground. I had lost my focus, and let my thick head get the better of me.

But if mistakes happen, it is always about… the next ball.

We reminded ourselves.

THE NEXT BALL!

THE BALL CAME in over the top and I went to side-step Casey, and fed it out to Quinn. We cleared it.

But as I released the ball, Casey had come in and hit me a belt.

I rolled over holding my back. The game was stopped, and Casey got a yellow card for his troubles. Dr Loftus came in to see if I was okay?

I told him I was just wasting time.

He started to laugh, but then told me to open my mouth… to let on he was having a look. He rubbed some water down my back. 'We're nearly there!' he then reminded me. 'Get up and let's finish this game!'

The clash bought us another two minutes.

Time was ticking. We were on the verge of glory as stoppage time began. Mayo had enjoyed plenty of the ball, and young McDonald got his second point to bring it back to two. That lad from Crossmolina turned out to be a handy player for them after that, to say the least, but this would not be his day.

I had a fair idea I was taking my last kick-out! I had gone route one all day long… driving it as long and as far as I could, aiming for the lads in the middle.

But I could see the midfield was crowded. Thirty yards down to my left, however, Joe Honeyman was standing on his own. I pinged the ball out to him for my first short kick-out ever.

He ran with it, fed it out to Mickey Quinn and Barney Breen got a hold of it… and Barney was fouled.

Aiden Rooney was standing over it.

Seamus turned to me with laughter across his face.

'WE HAVE IT!' he roared.

'WE F***ING HAVE IT!'

Rooney was told it was the last kick of the game, and Aiden smiled and gave a thumbs-up! He planted the ball on the ground and took his time.

Mick Curley blew his whistle as the ball sailed over the bar.

That was it.

History!

0-12 to 2-4.

STREAMS OF LEITRIM supporters flooded onto the field with their straw hats, flags and unbridled joy, as I fell to my knees and cried.

I absolutely bawled my eyes out.

Months of preparation had gone into this moment, and it had been a real rollercoaster of a day. From meeting up that morning to letting in a goal in the first few seconds!

I was so focused in the entire build-up.

I had channelled so much energy.

Now, all of those emotions just poured out of me.

I was on my knees for two minutes solid. Supporters crowded around me patting me on the back.

But I nearly wanted them to go away and leave me alone!

I just wanted to savour that moment for myself… until I joined what would be the party of all parties.

When I got up, finally, and looked around me I couldn't see a blade of grass. The pitch was just a sea of green and gold. It was a joy to behold.

The entire euphoria of what we had achieved really hit home. Every man, woman and child in our small county was having their day on top.

After the game I spoke to the media and told them that I had let in the goal at the start to give Mayo a chance, because I knew we were going to win… and I still stand by that!

Even if it is just me covering myself for the f**k-up of the early goal!

My brother was standing beside me on the field, proud as punch wearing jeans dyed in the Leitrim colours. All the scenes around me were just surreal; it seemed like the whole county was on the field. I think the *Leitrim Observer* had asked the last person to leave the county to turn off the lights that week.

I met my father outside the gate, because he wasn't able to come on to the field. He had literally shot himself in the foot a few weeks before the game, and that's no joke.

He did a bit of shooting, and whatever way he pulled the gun out from the front of the car, it went off and hit him in the foot.

He was in the stand on the day of the final, when some of the Mayo supporters had been pointing out how small the Leitrim goalkeeper was. But when I made that big save to deny Golding, someone asked them… 'How small is he now?!' And pointed out that my father was in their company.

I was told after the game they turned around and shook his hand, and congratulated him on my efforts on the field.

OUR SECOND CONNACHT championship! We had left everything on that field, so much so that Declan Darcy didn't even have to walk to the stand to lift the cup.

Our jubilant supporters carried him there on their shoulders like a king.

That day, we were all kings.

Getting back to the dressing-room took an age, but watching Declan go up to receive the cup was such a proud moment for him personally, for us as his teammates… and for every Leitrim person across the globe.

Our Connacht title-winning captain from 1927, Tom Gannon was there. He was 95 at the time! Tom passed away in 1998, but a priceless photo of both skippers was taken with the cup as they lifted it together. A special moment that will be treasured forever.

Fans and kids wanted us to sign programmes, jerseys, footballs… and one lad I knew from home asked me to sign his chest for the craic!

In the dressing-room, Johno came over and congratulated me. He had asked us to 'show him the cup'… and we obliged.

The Nestor Cup sat proudly in the middle of us all.

I reminded him of the night we trained in the snow. He had told us that evenings like that would win us a Connacht title, and he was right. Training in snow, muck and dirt across Leitrim, Kells, Forest Park and Strandhill was the making of the team and we had the prize to show for it.

We made all of those sacrifices to achieve something special, and it was worth it. Johno was always reserved and quiet in his own way, and wasn't one for going mental in the dressing-room if we won or lost.

He was always calm and collected, and never even flinched when the final whistle went that day. He was the same when he led Galway to their first of two All-Irelands four years later.

But in this moment, you could tell he was bursting with pride.

He always said he was there to do a job for the people of Leitrim, and boy did he do that.

He was well aware of Leitrim's passion for the game before he took the job, and wanted to really tap into that. There was something about that passion that drew him to the Leitrim manager's job, and that continued to drive him on.

Eventually, after a lifetime it seemed, we pulled away towards Carrick with the Nestor Cup on board. The radio was on while we were on the bus, and the whole bus roared laughing and cheering when my post-match interview came on.

The difference between getting on that bus in the morning… and leaving the Hyde as champions! When we got as far as the outskirts of Carrick an open-top bus was waiting for us. Only Johno, Joe and Ollie had known about it.

A convoy of hundreds of cars followed us on the bus into Carrick.

The excitement of getting on an open-top bus alone was huge, because I had never been on one before! It was another masterstroke from John and the management, because it allowed us to connect with the supporters without being swamped down on the packed streets below.

I'll never know what they would have done with the bus had we lost, but thankfully that gamble paid off as we toured victoriously through the town.

IT WAS HEADING for nightfall. We were all starving and, as we passed a pub, the owner landed out with crates of beer for us all – but I told him to go back and get me a Club Orange!

I never needed alcohol before, and I still didn't need it now.

We were crawling through the town. We went around it twice, as the place was going bananas. RTÉ were there filming it all for the evening news… and there I was waving around my can of Club Orange at the front of the bus going mad. The party went well into the Monday morning. I was exhausted, and as my daughter Emma was less than three months old at the time, I went home early enough. But I still made my usual stop at Jimmy O'Connor's in Dromod.

I never passed that place after a game… win, lose or draw… rain, hail or shine.

Of course, the place was wedged.

The roof nearly lifted when I walked in. Three lads lifted me up on their shoulders and carried me from the door to the rear of the pub… and back again.

There was time for another Club Orange or two in there.

On the Monday, I arrived back to Aughnasheelin. My father had put up a huge banner across our road saying, WELL DONE MARTIN… just to show off the place where I was reared more than anything!

The club had a big banner up too. The parish beamed with pride.

They were all proud of what I had achieved, and seeing those things filled me up with my own sense of achievement. I was a Leitrim hero now, but it starts at home with your club, and parish and neighbours. That massive family.

I hadn't been home that week at all, and didn't go to work on the Monday either… I don't think anyone did!

We went around every village and town that day, from morning until night with the cup, and we arrived in Ballinamore late on. It was lashing rain.

But even though it was so late and a rotten night, there were still people out in their hundreds to greet us.

IN THE AFTERMATH of it all, we were flat out going to functions and presentations to give out medals. One night I had to go to Cloone dressed up as St Patrick while wearing a mask.

They were raising funds, and I had to go around the pubs dressed as the man himself and people had to guess who I was.

One of the clues was… 'It's not always the bacon he saves.'

Only two people got it right!

I was guest of honour at a presentation night for my own club, and had to give a speech. I brought the cup with me, and I had to wait outside with it, all dressed up in my shirt and tie. When I was introduced and walked into the hall, hundreds of my own were there cheering and clapping. I told them about starting off at the old field in Shreheen with Pat Cull, and him asking me, 'Who we had for goals?'

For weeks and months afterwards people recognised us, and thanked us for the part we all played in that victory.

I work in Sligo University Hospital now, and deal with a lot of people who might be a bit confused. If they are from Leitrim, you use your slice of fame to talk about football and sport, and their faces will light up because they'll remember, or even tell you they were actually there that day.

Shannonside FM often hire me as a co-commentator for Leitrim matches, and I'm always introduced as a… *1994 Connacht champion.*

To go 67 years between titles was such a long time. The world was a very different place when Tom Gannon got hold of the Nestor Cup compared to when we did. Ireland was only born as a country, and the horrors of the Second World War were still a dozen years away.

In 1994, Charlie McGettigan and Paul Harrington won the Eurovision Song Contest for Ireland with *Rock 'n' Roll kids.* Jack Charlton was given the freedom of Dublin. And Bertie Ahern was elected leader of Fianna Fáil.

There were so many bad days for Leitrim football in between all of that. So many fabulous players never got to the top of that mountain, like the late Packy McGarty, Mickey Martin and our selector Ollie Honeyman. They all gave stellar service to Leitrim GAA and never got their Connacht medal.

HAVING THAT ONE medal is huge.

It's here in the house somewhere, along with my blue and gold jersey from that day… even if it might not fit me anymore. When my time comes, it would be nice to have the jersey on my coffin at least!

People of all ages, so many years later, are still talking about what we achieved. And I know it will live long in the memories forever.

« CHAPTER 8 »

THE TUESDAY AFTER the game, I went back to work, and lads were there banging the tables and roaring when we landed, to acknowledge what we had done.

There was chat galore about the game, the scenes after it and the celebrations that went on across the county over the course of those couple of days. There wasn't much work done.

The lads slagged me a bit about my mistake for Mayo's first goal too, but that didn't matter too much… my medal was secure.

For the Leitrim panel, the fun was over when we went back to training the Saturday after the Connacht final, and I'm fairly sure some of the lads were still a bit drunk when they turned up.

There wasn't a ball to be seen. Once again, lads were getting sick and bringing up their breakfast from that morning, including myself.

We ran ourselves into the ground… again!

And I was lapping lads I had never overtaken before in those long runs. It was only because they had such a heavy time partying and they were clearing out all of that dirty diesel.

They were sweating drink, while I was sweating chips and Club Orange!

The training remained severe for a few sessions, because the gap before the next game was three weeks… an All-Ireland semi-final at Croke Park.

What we had achieved was seismic. Everyone was still giddy and excited as the high from winning filtered through the squad and the county.

One night, when we were summoned to a training session in Kells, we were all told to wear our gear from the Connacht final for a squad photo with the Nestor Cup. At another session word surfaced that the Leitrim Association in New York wanted to fly us to the Big Apple as guests of honour later in the year, in October, and that was a nice little distraction too.

Lads were worrying about money, passports and all that craic. Johno didn't like it because our season was far from over, but it had to be done. Thankfully, we had to pay for nothing in the end!

All of the flights and accommodation were taken care of, and when we did arrive in the States at the end of that famous year, we had the time of our lives, and we were wined and dined like heroes returning 'home' from war. I had a steak dinner one night and, genuinely, there was half a cow on the plate. On top of that, we were all given an envelope with $100 inside to spend on ourselves.

FIRST, OUR FOCUS had shifted to the All-Ireland semi-final. We didn't know who we were going to be playing, but we did know it would be the Leinster champions. We played a few challenge games, and went about our business as normal once we dusted off the Connacht final cobwebs. The chips and pints were burned away again.

A week after our victory over Mayo, Dublin pipped a brilliant Meath team under Sean Boylan by a point at Croke Park in the Leinster decider, and star man Charlie Redmond scored 1-4.

Their attack was scary. They had Vinnie Murphy, Dessie Farrell, Mick Gavlin and then Brian Stynes was a giant in their midfield alongside Pat Gilroy. This was us against the big boys, the minnows against the kingpins… the culchies against the city slickers.

That was Dublin's third Leinster title in-a-row, but they were gunning for their first All-Ireland since 1983. Losing the 1992 final against Donegal had been a huge shock, but Sam Maguire was back within their sights and they looked like they really meant business under Pat O'Neill.

But we were a game away from an All-Ireland final – where no Leitrim team had gone before.

Croker could hold around 58,000 then, and building was already underway on the new Cusack Stand to turn it into the fantastic stadium we know it as today. We had to get our heads around all of this, so we went up the week beforehand at our leisure to watch the other All-Ireland semi-final between eventual winners Down and Cork.

The night before that match we got to walk out at Croke Park and go into the dressing-rooms we'd be in just to get a feel for the place. We stayed in The Burlington Hotel, and were all seated in the Cusack as the Mournemen progressed to the final with a 1-13 to 0-11 win against the Rebels.

Watching that game gave us a sense of the atmosphere and being at Croker with a full crowd, and there was black and amber everywhere. The lads started taking the piss, and Joe Honeyman started shouting 'Up Down' as he got in and out of his seat.

Johno loved seeing us have that sort of silly banter in that scenario because he knew it was only good for us as a group. That was another reason behind all the weekends away and talks. We trained together, went away together and even got sick together. Everything was done as one big family, and there was no big hero or a reliance on one individual player.

Everyone had a job to do. This was one unit – even when it came to taking the piss and having a laugh before things got serious.

Down had that too. Pete McGrath had a serious team, and Gary Mason scored six points that day. They were such a stylish side and had the likes of Mickey Linden in their attack along with Greg McCartan and Ross Carr. They also had been here and done it, because they were All-Ireland champions in 1991. Colin Corkery was excellent for the Rebels and scored one more point than Mason – seven in total – but it wasn't enough to beat a team so battle-hardend from the Ulster Championship.

Down's 1-14 to 1-12 Ulster quarter-final win over 1993 champions Derry that summer is considered to be one of the greatest championship games of all time.

The week flew by as we got our final preparations into place to take on the mighty Dubs. The night before the game we went up to the capital again and stayed in The Grand Hotel in Malahide.

This was long before the M4 was built, so when we pulled out of Carrick we had to go through every town and village on the way until we got to the big smoke. Every place we passed had Leitrim flags up to greet us on our way to Dublin, which added hugely to the excitement ahead of the biggest game of our lives.

They were standing out for us all through Longford, and when we passed through Kells, where we trained, they were out in force for us there too, which was no surprise given how intense the Dublin-Meath rivalry was at the time.

I was sharing a room with Martin Prior, and we just chilled out for a while. We had a little kick-about that evening before our dinner and team-talk. Apart from that, we just relaxed; nobody was too wound-up.

There was a nice buzz, because we were the Connacht champions going to Croke Park. We were there on merit, and all of the pressure was on Dublin. Johno certainly didn't put any pressure on us. He didn't approach it as if this was the be-all and end-all. If we performed well, we could cause a shock, but if we didn't... so be it.

He never tapped into the whole underdogs' thing too much either. There were only three teams left in the championship and we were one of them, so we had a free shot at it. We had absolutely nothing to lose.

We knew we were up against it, of course we were. Nobody gave us a chance, but we knew if we really hit our peak, there was no reason why we couldn't pull off a massive shock. As the team bus left the hotel on the Sunday morning for the game, we were accompanied by a Garda escort car and two motorbikes to guide us through the north of the city and into Drumcondra.

Johno had organised full suits and Leitrim polo-shirts for us to wear to make sure we looked like a team, and not individuals. He was always thinking ahead. As we came down the N1 through Whitehall, you could see all the traffic ahead of us moving to let the bus through, and we flew through every red light we met.

As we passed St Patrick's College and The Skylon Hotel, and got close to Quinn's pub on the Drumcondra Road, all you could see were Leitrim supporters. They were *everywhere!* I could feel my palms soaking with sweat and my heart rate started going through the roof, just as, who else... but Tina Turner came on the radio to sing us into Croker.

I was waving out the window to people I recognised and smiling at them, but I was absolutely s****ing blocks at the same time as the stadium came into view on Clonliffe Road.

THIS WAS SOMETHING I would never experience again in my life.

It was a proud moment. Leitrim in an All-Ireland semi-final as Connacht champions – it had only happened once before, it hasn't happened since and might never happen again.

We got into our dressing-room underneath the Hogan Stand. Galway were playing The Dubs in the minor match as our own Seamus Prior – who refereed the 1991 final between Down and Meath – was interviewed pitch-side by Marty Morrissey.

We were allowed out to watch some of it, and we filed into the front row of the Hogan Stand just inside the wire, all kitted out in full suits in the soaring heat. It was still over two hours before throw-in, but even our arrival there sparked a roaring welcome as a huge Leitrim contingent were already inside waiting for the big one.

The Tribesmen won the minor game by three points with a young fella from Killererin by the name of Padraic Joyce lighting up their attack.

A good few thousand were in the stadium already during that game, and I noticed a few people I knew in the Hogan Stand so I got up to go over and say hello. But as soon as I left my seat, Johno called me back to sit with my teammates. I presume he just wanted us to stick together and avoid any chit-chat with supporters before the match.

I didn't even know it, but my granny McHugh had died the night before and he was actually afraid one of them would sympathise with me and I'd find out. He didn't want me to know she had passed away before our match began, and I only found out about it after the game when we were back at the hotel afterwards.

George O'Rourke, an old classmate of mine came up to me and said, 'Hard luck in the game, and sorry to hear about your granny'.

It was a conscious decision by Johno to stop me mingling with the supporters in case I would hear the news. My family decided to shield me from her passing as well. It was just another example of Johno having eyes and ears everywhere. That wouldn't happen today but there were no mobile phones back then, never mind the internet!

But it didn't annoy me that I wasn't told before the match. Of course, I was upset when I found out she had passed away, but I had known she was sick. I didn't even know my family weren't at the match.

But that didn't matter as the day passed me by anyway. The nerves and the occasion got to me big-time. It was a beautiful sunny day, ideal for championship football. There is no other place on earth you would rather be, but I let myself get too wound-up.

I was just too focused.

I got wrapped up in it all, and it's a big regret when I look back now all of these years later.

The craic was the usual in the dressing-room when we got in to tog out, and we actually waited a little longer when The Dubs were already out on the field as Johno got in his final word before the 3.30 throw-in. The game was also live on TV, so the eyes of the country were on us.

When we ran out from the old tunnel where the Canal End met the old Hogan Stand, we were greeted by this unmerciful cheer. That was the moment you realised... *This isn't Carrick, Tuam Stadium or the Hyde!*

Our supporters went absolutely berserk as we lined up for a pre-match photo. Again, I stood at the back, flanked by the giants and you can actually see the nerves across my face. We went down to warm up by the old Canal End which was awash with Leitrim supporters.

The hairs on the back of my neck were standing up!

This was the only time I ever let the whole occasion get to me. Even before the match started, my head was down. I was uptight and shouting at myself inside saying... *Come on ta f**k!! Cop on and get in the zone!!*

I was just too wrapped up in it, I felt everything had to be perfect... and the size of the crowd didn't help either. Hill 16 was wedged with expectant Dubs and their usual noise and colour.

Leitrim had a population of 25,000, and 52,606 were there to see how we'd get on in the lion's den... and I just f**king froze. I riled myself too much, and got myself into a tizzy for one of the biggest games I would ever play in.

If I'd do it all over again, I'd be far more relaxed and I make a point of doing just that in every game I have played since then.

We got into our positions behind the Artane Band for the parade... I got in behind Declan Darcy as usual. He'd be back here plenty of times in his career, but this was a monumental day for him too. He grew up as a Dub, and switched to play with them in 1998. He was a selector when they won six All-Irelands under

Jim Gavin – and was a vital cog in their famous five in-a-row in 2019 and his transition into a brilliant coach never surprised me.

But in 1994 Dublin were not that force just yet, and were trying to end their 11-year wait for the big one. The expectancy with them was always huge. They were close, but always just fell short when it came to the crunch.

Back in the parade, I was taking in deep breaths and ignoring the euphoric crowd with my head down. I never bothered looking up, and refused to soak up the atmosphere as two-thirds of Croke Park was green and gold.

I just did the whole thing wrong, and it cost me and the nerves never went away as *Amhrán na bhFiann* rang out around Croke Park and legends like Tom Gannon and Packie McGarty looked on from the stands in hope.

WHEN KERRY'S TOMMY Sugrue threw in the ball, the Dubs kicked a few early wides from Charlie Redmond, Jack Sheedy and Vinnie Murphy.

It was only early doors, but that really helped myself and my full-back line of Fergal Reynolds, Seamus Quinn and Joe Honeyman take a few deep breaths and settle a bit. Seamus in particular would go on to have a monstrous performance for us, and just three minutes in he dived in and blocked down a Mick Galvin effort like *Superman*. Redmond put over the resulting '45' for the first score of the game. Seamus deservedly got an All Star for us that year – himself and Mickey Quinn are the only Leitrim men who have ever won one.

Noel Moran got a brilliant score for us into the Hill to settle us down and briefly silence the famous old terrace. But, shortly after that, with just eight minutes on the clock, I was called into action when Farrell played Galvin in on goal, and his shot was straight at me from point-blank range much to my relief.

My nerves were bad enough, without having to pick the ball out of my net so early for the second big match in-a-row.

Aiden Rooney and Darcy put us 0-3 to 0-1 ahead, and just for a moment our supporters could dare to dream as Farrell kicked another wide past my posts and into the terrace. Then, just 15 minutes in, Dublin did hit the net. Redmond played a neat one-two with Farrell, and even though it looked like he initially over-carried it and it looked like Farrell threw it back to him, he blasted it past me to make it 1-2 to 0-3. Murphy fisted one over the bar for his second of the day, as Galvin and Redmond sent the Dubs 1-5 to 0-3 clear.

Aiden Rooney ended what felt like an eternity for our next point when he tapped over a free but we were already up against it. Dublin were just coasting along.

John O'Leary's kick-outs were huge for them, even though we did win possession off a few of them but we were failing to make it count.

Redmond was through on goal but, again, Seamus Quinn made a remarkable block to save our bacon. Dublin were screaming for a penalty amid claims Seamus used his foot, but they worked the ball back out to Farrell who swung it between the posts for his first point. It was starting to look bad for us.

They just kept picking away at us for the rest of the half, until they pulled eight clear on the stroke of half-time with a brilliant team goal.

O'Leary took hold of a wayward Paul Kieran kick. Dermot Deasy, Paddy Moran, Galvin, Niall Guiden and Deegan were all involved and Galvin kept his run going to lash into the top corner.

Our chance of a fairytale was up in smoke.

There were seven passes between O'Leary getting it and Galvin scoring to make it 2-7 to 0-5. It was the goal of the year, but I felt I could have done more to prevent it. It was just another example of the occasion getting to me. Seamus had a brilliant game as did Noel Moran and a few others, but I think the occasion got to a lot of the lads. Salt was rubbed into our wounds when George Dugdale had to be physically carried off by two medics at half-time with a bad ankle injury and was replaced by Barney Breen.

Johno insisted we were not out of it yet and to keep fighting, even though we had that sucker-punch just before the break.

IN THE SECOND-HALF, Dublin kept chipping away at the scoreboard and Redmond was at the core of the danger in their attack. He really seemed to motor when he was playing into an adoring Hill 16, and soon enough he sent them 10 points in front.

2-10 to 0-6.

Niall Guiden and Paul Bealin stretched Dublin's lead even further, before Colin McGlynn scored Leitrim's first ever goal in a championship match at Croke Park when Barney brilliantly played him in. Our fans enjoyed the moment, and they deserved it!.

But the Dubs responded when Farrell took the ball around me and scored their third goal… and I buried my head in my hands. Redmond finished with 1-6 that day. Their attack was just on fire. All of their inside forwards got goals.

We shook hands with them and wished them luck in the final, and I couldn't get over how big O'Leary was when I approached him. My hand going into his was like a spade going into a shovel.

They were into the final and they looked like champions to me, but Down had the last laugh in the decider a month later. The result didn't stop our supporters from flooding on to the field in appreciation of the journey we had brought them on, but we were bitterly disappointed. We hadn't kept the dream alive.

Colm O'Rourke said on *The Sunday Game* that the result proved Connacht football was well behind the rest, after Mayo had also lost the 1993 semi-final heavily to Cork, but we didn't feel that way.

The dressing-room was filled with disappointment and a few reporters were speaking to us, and as we came out to head for the bus plenty of Leitrim supporters were still around. They were proud of how far we had come and what we had accomplished for such a small county, and that put a smile back on my face, as I was still very annoyed with myself for letting the game pass me by.

I felt I didn't do myself any justice, but meeting those supporters helped boost my spirits again. Everyone knew we were up against it; nobody had expected anything and a Connacht title was huge.

Uncles of mine had come from England and America to go to Croke Park, and hundreds of other Leitrim people flew in from all over the world to be there. It was just incredible.

After the game we were late for our meal at the hotel because we had spent so much time talking to neighbours, friends and relatives… people deserving of our time after the game.

The hotel was buzzing with Leitrim people. In their eyes, we were still heroes. To them, we were heroes forever because that's what winning a Connacht championship meant.

When I was about to head to bed, that's when I heard about my poor granny off George O'Rourke to bring a really sombre end to the weekend.

It was back to the club after that, and we were still signing autographs at games and people were still congratulating us on the Connacht title. Suddenly, there wasn't a word about the Dublin game at all.

But having played at Croke Park in front of that many people made it hard at times to switch focus back to the club and playing in front of a couple of hundred in Division 2. A lot of us were still attending functions at this stage as well, and all of these things side-tracked us. The cup was still going around the county to presentations and schools and wherever else people asked for it… from weddings to funerals, birthday parties to wakes.

I think everyone in the county got to hold it at some stage over the course of the year.

When I was playing underage football, Brian Stafford came to present us with medals one year when Meath were All-Ireland champions, and at the time I thought it was huge. Now, we were in that sort of limelight having achieved something major that Leitrim people may never see again.

It was important that we didn't turn anything or anyone down. I loved signing autographs and jerseys and whatever else it was we had to do in return for all of that remarkable support we received.

It made me feel that all of my hard work had paid off, going back to that day in the kitchen in 1982 watching Martin Furlong on that little TV minding the sticks at the very spot where I finally stood myself on that hallowed ground.

THINGS WEREN'T GOING great with Aughnasheelin, but it still meant a lot to me to return there and there wasn't much of a break until the 1994/1995 National League campaign with Leitrim was upon us.

We were in Division 2, but we had the Connacht champions tag now and Galway and Mayo were both in our division as well. They were out to settle a few early scores. All eyes were on us, and the trip to New York was coming thick and fast at the start of October. We were fitted with new blazers as 23 of us descended on the Big Apple.

Our sponsors, the McGovern brothers of Aughavas played a huge role in getting us over there, and Mike Carty looked after us all at Rosie O'Grady's pub smack bang in the middle of Manhattan.

We went to more functions, and there was plenty of sightseeing, along with a challenge game against New York before hitting home – as our first league match against Tyrone in Carrick beckoned.

The legs were heavy, but we beat them by a point – 1-7 to 0-9 – and we gradually got back at it in terms of the intensity at training and getting our fitness back up to scratch. Clare hammered us 1-9 to 0-4 in Ennis in the second round. We failed to score from play.

But even though we lost, I made one of the saves of the year!

A high ball came in on top of Seamus Quinn.

David Keane let fly... it was heading for the top corner, and I must have jumped about four feet into the air to my left... and put it out for a '45'.

We redeemed ourselves two weeks later when we beat Galway 0-9 to 0-6 in Carrick. But the off-field distractions were still going strong. A gang of us went to London as guests of the Leitrim Association over there for their dinner dance. People jumped on the bandwagon offering us this, that and the other, but we didn't care one bit. Most importantly, we kept producing results on the field too. We all but assured ourselves of Division 2 status in November, when we beat Mayo 0-13 to 1-7 in Charlestown to finish the year on a high with three wins... all against our rivals in Connacht.

The result in Mayo was all the sweeter because we did it without the Aughawillan lads – Declan Darcy, Mickey Quinn and Gerry Flanagan who were in Connacht Club Championship action against Tuam Stars the following week.

Johno made sure we still trained all through the Christmas period and there was no real let-up heading into 1995.

Back then, January was usually free from inter-county action, but the new Connacht FBD League was starting, so there was no rest for the wicked. In our first ever FBD League match, we made it three wins in-a-row against Roscommon with a 2-7 to 0-11 victory in Cloone in the muck and dirt of the new year.

We drew with Galway in the second round but, more importantly... we finally got our Connacht winners' medals that month.

Mayo have 47 Connacht titles, but for us to win one was like finding a big lump of gold out in the garden.

It's something that might never happen again. I was officially a Connacht champion with Leitrim and the medal made it real.

All those months later I was on top of the world, but it wasn't long before it all came crashing down again.

PART **FOUR**

Those Three Words

Lining out for Dynamo Rooskey at different stages during my GAA career was a welcome break, as the less pressurised environment and the fun of the games were good for my head.

I look back on my career and am thrilled to be able to say I got to work with some of the greatest managers in Irish sport. This included John O'Mahony, and also a young Stephen Kenny (above) when he was boss at Longford Town, and later when I went down the coaching route myself, I got to link up with the brilliant Eamonn Coleman at both Gowna and also with the Cavan senior team.

« CHAPTER 9 »

MY FATHER DIED August 7, 1995. He had been complaining of a massive headache, but being a *typical* man, he just took tablets and thought nothing of it. He presumed it was nothing serious, that a few painkillers would make it go away.

He eventually went to Dr John Bourke in Ballinamore, who knew on the spot this was more than a headache, so dad was rushed off to Beaumont Hospital in Dublin for an emergency procedure.

We all drove down that morning. We were told the operation was complete, but there was bleeding on the brain. After a while we went in to see him, and the looks coming from the doctors weren't good. Daddy gave us a small thumb's up and a bit of a smile, but the next few hours were critical.

He took a turn for the worst. He became brain-dead, and he slipped away on us. It was very upsetting, because he was such a pillar in all of our lives.

The way he worked around the house and on the farm, he always pulled and dragged me along with him and he made me strong physically and mentally. He taught me the value of working hard and helping others.

I thank my father for the man I am today… including being a thick-ass!

His organs were donated, so at least we know he has still helped others after his death. That was him all over; he would have been delighted with that. When he worked at home and on the farm, he was always straight out to help a friend or a neighbour if they needed it and insisted no one around him wanted for anything.

Losing him was a big blow for all of us, but despite the pain of his death there was always time to crack a stupid joke to lighten the humour in our darkest hour. My brothers JJ or Pete would always say something smart, but they would always say it in a way to make everyone else laugh.

Even when dad's coffin was leaving the house for the funeral, as we were all consoling each other in a huddle, Pete shouted… 'AND… BREAK!'

As if we were in the middle of a timeout on a basketball court!

He had his way of cracking a little joke just to make light of a desperately sad situation.

But the support we got from everyone was immense. There was an enormous crowd at the funeral, and it just goes to show what people thought of him as a man. It was only then that we realised the amount of people he knew and how highly regarded he was. But that's how life is sometimes, and things got easier with time.

I HAD A match with the club a week or two after he passed away. The game was on in Ballinamore, and I insisted on playing in it. Dad would have wanted that too.

I wore a black armband as a mark of respect to the man who came to all of my matches for so many years, for both club and county, across Leitrim and beyond.

Playing that game, and football in general, really helped me get over his death and start that path to normality in a way, but his passing was a huge turning point in my life.

THE CHAMPIONSHIP STARTED in June against Galway in Carrick and all eyes were on us as defending Connacht champions.

We dominated the game, and I didn't have much to do.

Seamus was having a stormer in front of me, as he always did, and we were leading 0-7 to 0-6 at half-time. Padraig McGovern had put us two in front, but three minutes from time everything just unravelled and fell apart.

Padraig Kenny had been having a brilliant game marking Sean Óg de Paor, but was replaced with the match still in the melting pot. Ja Fallon brought it back to a point, before de Paor bombed up the field to curl a beauty over the bar and dump us out.

A 0-12 to 0-11 defeat to end our campaign.

You could hear a pin drop amongst the Leitrim supporters. We were the reigning champions, and expectations were high, but now the defence of our title was over before it had even started.

Seamus had actually planned on retiring from county football that year, but had been convinced to stay on because he knew we left a serious chance behind us.

Our team in 1995 was even stronger than the year before, and had we beaten Galway that day we definitely would have been Connacht champions again. Despite what people felt about the state of Connacht football at the time, who knows what would have happened after that in an All-Ireland semi-final against Tyrone.

A lot of people around Leitrim felt we would have taken care of them too – which would have meant an All-Ireland final against our old pals Dublin! *Imagine that?*

Hindsight is a great thing, and we'll never know. But such was the cruelty of knockout football. There was no safety net, and the entire summer was up in smoke, as Dublin did end their famine and get their hands on Sam Maguire.

It was nice to see their goalkeeper John O'Leary going up to lift the cup, because he had soldiered with them for so long.

The fact that we had played so well against Galway and lost so late in the match was such a bitter pill to swallow. But Johno backed us, as he always did, and told the press afterwards that we had won together, and we would lose together too… and he vowed to stay on for another year in charge.

BUT BY 1996, everything started to get a bit stale.

It wasn't Johno's fault, but sometimes a change is just needed.

Some players hung up their boots. The team just hit a wall. We could feel it all through the year, even though we maintained our Division 2 status again. Then, it was Galway again in the Connacht semi-final, where another brave performance counted for nothing.

The Tribe sent us packing 2-13 to 2-11 in Tuam, and once again we stared at the rest of the summer wondering where it all went wrong?

The team had reached the end of the road, and Johno bid us farewell to signal the end of a wonderful era for Leitrim football that may never be repeated.

And the real slide started from there.

Seamus Bonner came in after Johno for the 1997 season… and that's all he lasted.

Seamus had been involved when his native Donegal won the 1992 All-Ireland, and he had Pat O'Neill in with him too in an advisory role. Pat had just led the Dubs to the holy grail in 1995.

On paper it looked like a dream ticket, but it was a total disaster. It was just a poor campaign from start to finish, even though the league was kind to us again and we held our own in Division 2.

But trouble was bubbling under the surface, and it all nearly boiled over when we had a very lucky escape in London.

WE NEEDED EXTRA-TIME to beat the Exiles in Ruislip, and we really struggled – including myself. The pitch was like tarmac and my kick-outs were all over the place.

London were making hay as a result, and it took us over 20 minutes to score. We were 0-6 to 0-1 down at half-time!

A very dubious penalty came our way to see us level the game at the death, as we stared defeat in the face. Darcy saved our blushes and ended up scoring 2-11, but we had barely avoided the unthinkable and a hugely embarrassing result.

We didn't deserve to win the game and we were absolutely blessed to come home with the win. Massive cracks were starting to appear across the panel and a downward spiral was well underway.

Seamus was always going to be up against it following in John O'Mahony's steps, but the differences between the two men as managers was chalk and cheese. Training wasn't good enough… and it never started on time.

I'd often be there a bit early, but I was always left standing there wondering where everyone was? There was a really bad vibe about the place. Mayo were waiting to deliver the knockout punch in the 'semis' and they comfortably beat us by seven points to end another hugely disappointing campaign.

Bonner was straight out the door… and then it was Peter McGinnity's turn to try and turn the tide. He was a Fermanagh legend, and won an All Star in 1982 when they reached the Ulster final that year.

Peter was a totally different character again, and was very ruthless. He wanted things his way, or you went out the door. If you made a mistake, he'd let you know about it, and he took no nonsense. A player called Adrian Charles had joined the panel the year before, and he was working late one night and couldn't get off for training.

McGinnity told him if he didn't turn up, not to come back and there was no room for manoeuvre with him. But it seemed a bit needless and over the top at times.

Maybe O'Mahony's shadow still hung over the squad a bit too. We had reached a Connacht final and won it under a manager who wanted the best for us. The best was yet to come for Johno, who of course led Galway to the All-Ireland that year and landed another for them in 2001.

Johno had raised the bar for us but anyone who came in after that never met those standards. Peter was a good manager and a good player, but his attitude was just too ruthless, even though this was inter-county football.

BY THE END of 1998 I had enough.

I was getting tired. I had put my body through a lot since coming into the senior squad and I just didn't like how things materialised for Leitrim after Johno left.

I remember sitting on the bench one day when we were losing a league game against Westmeath, which I didn't mind.

A player I'll not name was asked to warm-up, but he said he had a sore leg. There was nothing wrong with him, he simply didn't want to play, it seemed to me. That was just one example of the direction things were going in.

So, I decided to bow out gracefully after Peter's first year… and that was that. I was still working in the factory but I wasn't happy there either and needed a career change too.

Life was taking over and pulling me in too many directions. I was getting stressed out over stupid things and I eventually left my job at the meat factory in 2001 and started working as a painter and decorator.

But my door on sport still wasn't closed… it never was and I don't think it ever will be.

Playing senior football for Leitrim meant there wasn't much time for anything else, but I always enjoyed playing soccer from my time with Dynamo Rooksey before I got that life changing call-up from Johno.

But when I stepped away from county football, I got involved with Dynamo again, before a stint with Longford Wanderers saw me end up with Longford Town's 'B' team. It was ideal for the winter, and I loved it. And ahead of the 1998/99 season, I got called up to their senior League of Ireland squad as a back-up keeper to their new signing Stephen O'Brien.

O'Brien was only the same height as me, but would become a legend at the club and is still their record appearance holder in the League of Ireland.

He spent time with Gillingham in his youth and was on the bench for Shelbourne when they played Rangers in the UEFA Cup shortly before his move to the midlands. To put it simply, he was an outstanding goalkeeper.

It's funny how, when you are getting a few pounds for it, you are happy enough to sit on the bench! But the whole experience of being there and seeing how the manager worked was a real eye-opener.

THE GAFFER WAS a young 26-year-old from Dublin by the name of Stephen Kenny. He was a very astute and professional man, and I can see why he got where he did in his career.

Anyone who was late got fined £1.

Anyone who had dirty boots had to cough up £2. It all added to the banter and the money pot that the club needed every penny from. Every manager is different in their approach and how they deal with players. With PJ Carroll and the Leitrim under-21s it was laps, laps… sprinting and laps. Johno had his rigid planning and man-management skills and made Leitrim football important, and took us to a place we never thought we would go. But those who replaced him in Leitrim had their own way or the highway, which myself and plenty of others didn't like.

But Stephen Kenny was totally different again. Obviously, it's a different sport, but he had a very unique way of looking at games even at this young age.

He had different training, motivation and preparation – even for a goalkeeper. I developed even more skills in terms of coming for crosses, diving, handling and having the ball at my feet.

You don't have all that in gaelic football, but when I did return to it a year later, my time in a professional environment drove my own standards up a few notches and it helped me hugely.

I was far more alert coming out for a high ball and stuff like that, and I realised that any time I was diving, I was physically jumping backwards!

So, all of that was rectified through specific goalkeeping coaching, which I had never experienced before. My GAA background stood well to me in other areas, and I could kick the ball the length of the shorter pitch! If we went route one, I was actually often able to assist a goal or two and the managers loved that.

There was a different type of atmosphere in the Longford Town squad, and a different type of pressure.

For a start, the league season in the First Division alone was 36 matches, so the games were on top of you all season long. Kenny still ran hard training sessions, but they were all ball-work. The players would go off and do short, sharp drills with the ball before we all linked up again later in the session. It was fiercely competitive but very enjoyable.

Myself and Stephen O'Brien would go off and do our own work, and as I said it was the first time I was ever pulled aside from the rest of the squad to be properly coached as a goalkeeper.

Even though I was on the bench, I enjoyed it because it was just totally different, and I learned so much from O'Brien. I did get to play a few times when Stephen was injured, and faced the likes of Home Farm Everton and Shelbourne. But I was No 1 for the 'B' team and lined out against the likes of Shamrock Rovers and Bohemians in the reserve division.

Stephen was so professional in what he was doing.

He would talk about the opposition first, and would go through various tactics if we were defending corners or free-kicks in huge detail… everyone had a job to do. We finished fourth in the First Division and I made two appearances, but you could see Stephen was a special man working on something special too.

He led them to promotion a year later and brought them to the 2001 FAI Cup final, which they lost to Bohemians, and Kenny subsequently took over the Gypsies at Dalymount Park.

But Longford built on those foundations to lift the cup a year later, and again in 2004.

Stephen's star continued to rise and took him all the way to be manager of the Republic of Ireland team and he is building a very exciting young side, even though he was under early pressure when they failed to qualify for the 2022 World Cup.

IT JUST GOES to show, you never know the path anyone can take.

I had no idea who Peter Canavan was when I faced him for the Leitrim under-21s, or who Ciaran McDonald was when he came off the Mayo bench against us in the 1994 Connacht final.

They were all stars starting to rise, and would all become household names.

I remember saving a shot from Joe Brolly in a league game against Derry one year, and he turned around and said, 'How the f**k did you save that?' It was a good question. He didn't get his goal that day, but Joe has done alright for himself too.

Playing with or against so many players over the years and being under the watch of so many managers, you just never knew where anyone could end up – there are plenty of other lads I played with and against whose sporting dreams didn't go in the direction they would have liked.

But I'm proud to say I played under the future Irish manager, and played against some of the greats of gaelic football too.

« CHAPTER 10 »

I WAS STILL living in Newtownforbes in Longford at this point, and Clonguish were in my ear about joining them. They were going all-out for a county title.

They hadn't won one since 1981.

I kept turning them down out of loyalty to Aughnasheelin, even though we were going *nowhere* and winning *nothing*.

Travelling home for training and games was my duty, and I would have found it very hard to leave my home club again after that brief stint with Kilglass Gaels in 1991.

They never twisted my arm to play for them that year, but I did start to get involved in coaching with their under-16s and minor teams, and we won a lot with them. It gave me a feel for management and I was just teaching myself as I went. But I got a great taste for it, and I liked the challenge of it and taking charge on the training field.

The winning feeling you get as a manager is special too, and I got involved as manager of St Brigid's Killashee in Longford as well, an intermediate club. We won all of our league games and were crowned champions. I was able to put my own stamp on things, pick the team I wanted and exert my influence on the squad.

I ploughed my own furrow but used all the little nuggets I got from John O'Mahony and the other various coaches and managers I played for in gaelic football and soccer.

I absolutely loved it.

I barked on the sideline as much as I did when I was on the field! But the lads responded to me, and thankfully it told with the results.

We got to an intermediate county final with Killashee in 2001, but lost to Carrickedmond. On the same day at Pearse Park, my Clonguish under-16s were in the county final as well two hours beforehand and won, so it was a busy day of mixed emotions to say the least!

It was a long day at the office, but it was nice to be involved that way and I was extremely proud of both teams.

All the while, only 12 or 13 lads were turning up to training at home and that was demoralising after those drives back home to train and be greeted by very few bodies. And we were losing a lot of matches.

ALL THE WHILE, Clonguish seniors were still in my ear.

They had over 30 at their training sessions and had the likes of Longford legend Paul Barden, Enda Williams and Paddy Dowd in their impressive squad. They were on the march to do something special.

All they were missing was a goalkeeper.

But I still felt a loyalty to the club at home despite the big appeal to make that switch and achieve something in club championship football. In the meantime, I got a phone call out of the blue from Pat Donoghue's brother Gary to come over to Gowna in Cavan and help out with some coaching for their goalkeeper Ronan Bannon.

He needed work on his kick-outs and reflexes, and a bit of fine-tuning. Their manager was the late great Eamonn Coleman, who led Derry to the promised land in 1993. I said I would go up, but asked myself... *What the f**k do I know about coaching keepers?!* I hadn't a clue about how to do specific work with a goalie, bar what I knew myself.

Eamonn was a lovely man. He lived in Gowna at the time and was incredibly welcoming. I was introduced to Ronan; we had a chat and ran through a few drills. I was learning on the job, but Ronan enjoyed it and liked what I was doing. Before I knew it, I was back for every session after that, putting him through his paces.

And myself and Eamonn had one thing in common straightaway – we were both roaring lunatics.

Eamonn would be there shouting away in his thick northern accent and I'd be down at the other end of the pitch screaming away in my own Leitrim one. The people in the parish must have thought there was blue murder going on at the club every night we trained.

They had a lot of decent players, and Cavan legend Dermot McCabe was one of their main men – an All Star winner from their Ulster Championship winning side in 1997. Bernard Morris was another hero in the county and he was like a block with legs on it, and these lads were proven winners who had won back-to-back Cavan titles in 2000.

The training with Aughnasheelin gradually decreased as I had my commitments with Gowna, and they reached the 2002 county final against Cavan Gaels. On the exact same day, Clonguish were in the Longford decider against Ballymahon – and in the back of my head I thought of the transfer that never was and the prospect of a senior championship medal... because I was nearly 32.

My focus was on Breffni Park, and Eamonn reminded me of Johno the way he had everything planned out, and how good he was with his players.

You could see why he delivered Derry's only All-Ireland senior title with the likes of Fergal McCusker, Anthony Tohill, Tony Scullion and Kieran McKeever.

He had the team bus sorted, and the players wanted for nothing. Dermot McCabe stood up on the way to the game and made an unmerciful speech to rally the troops.

A few of their players were on the wrong side of 30, and Dermot told them it was all or nothing... it was their last shot at it. I spent the entire second half on the 20-metre line, barking away at Ronan and he listened to every word, in fairness to him!

They didn't let that chance pass them by, and won their sixth title in nine seasons. Dermot was true to his word, because they haven't won it since. I was left wondering if I would ever get my own medal.

Less than 30 miles down the road, Clonguish had lost the Longford final by two points.

But that result made my decision for me. I transferred to Clonguish for the 2003 campaign with an eye on that medal because I knew how close they were, and things at Aughnasheelin were showing no signs of getting better.

If anything, they were getting worse.

SOME PEOPLE IN the parish were disappointed with my decision, but others understood. I was driving back from Newtownforbes to train, and leaving a young family I wanted to tend to! And only a handful of people were showing up to train.

I wanted more success with the end of the road in sight, and just wanted to make life that bit easier and cut out the travelling. I had to do it for myself really.

At Clonguish, Mick McCormack was in charge. He was an old-school manager, and loved giving us long runs and laps. He didn't know who I was and put me in at corner-back in a game at my first training session.

F**k it, I thought to myself, but I was only in the door and didn't want to rock the boat by telling him I didn't play out the field. Thankfully, one of the lads piped up and said I was a goalkeeper!

I gradually integrated into the group and got to know who was who. Paul Barden needed no introduction but they had a lot of great players and I settled in really well. They loved my long, thumping kick-outs and they couldn't get over the distance I could get on them despite my size.

We won the league, won the Leader Cup and got back to the county final against Ballymahon. Clonguish still hadn't won a county title since 1981, and revenge was on the cards from the defeat the year before when I looked on... from Cavan.

I got the perception from my teammates and the management that the missing link was a goalkeeper.

As we filed in behind the band for the pre-match parade at Pearse Park, my mind was taken right back to the 1994 All-Ireland semi-final against Dublin at Croker – the day I let myself choke and the game totally passed me by.

This wasn't Croker or an All-Ireland semi-final but I kept thinking about that day, and I was so determined not to let this one pass me by. This was my first senior championship final and I had to make it count. You never know when these chances will come at you again.

I soaked up the atmosphere and relaxed, and looked up at the crowd and gave the odd thumbs-up to the terrace. I gave the middle finger to another fella I knew, who was laughing at me and it sparked a few cheers and bursts of laughter from both sets of supporters.

We drew 0-11 to 1-8 in a really scrappy game, but we hammered them 0-11 to 1-1 in the replay in awful conditions – the scoreline sums that up!

We won the lot that year, and it was great to be back at the top and finally tick those boxes as a club player. Winning the county title meant a Leinster Club Championship campaign, and we started off with a brilliant win over Wexford champions Kilanerin.

We backed it up when we sent Meath kingpins Blackhall Gaels packing in the quarter-finals to set up a daunting semi-final against the Dublin champions St Brigid's.

They had Rory and Raymie Gallagher in their attack, and they had too much for us in a 2-11 to 3-6 win in Mullingar.

It was a brilliant game, and I remember Seamus and Barry McWeeney came down from Aughnasheelin to support me in it. That really meant a lot to me.

Who came off the bench for them in the second-half, only my old skipper Declan Darcy, and they had Kenneth Darcy and Jason Ward from Leitrim as well. They went on to win the Leinster title against Round Towers of Kildare.

Our season was over, but in 2004 we won the league and championship again just to nail down our dominance in Longford. We destroyed Father Manning Gaels 1-15 to 0-5 in the county final in a perfect performance.

Suddenly, my medal tally was clocking up and we were going for the three in-a-row. But we were well beaten 3-10 to 0-8 by Offaly club giants Rhode at the first hurdle in Leinster. But we just got cocky heading into the 2005 campaign.

Effort levels dropped and we failed to even make the final. Dromard were crowned champions. Our attitude dipped; you could see lads making excuses to dodge training and not put in the effort to retain the title. For the talent that we had, we should have won more.

IN THE MIDDLE of all this, Eamonn Coleman became the Cavan senior manager in 2003, and he brought me with him to work with the goalkeepers.

One of the coaches was Martin McElkennon and I learned so much from him. He is a Tyrone man who worked with Mickey Harte when he was over their minor team, and would also go on to train Monaghan and Meath with Seamus 'Banty' McEnaney.

It's amazing what I was learning and picking up moving from all these training sessions, and coaches and managers, and just educating myself as I went along.

One weekend, when Cavan had no game, we trained on the Saturday evening and had another session on the Sunday morning, so myself and Martin booked into The Kilmore Hotel. It was all courtesy of the county board, of course.

We landed for the second training session and there was a doctor at the door to take urine samples off all the players.

I had never heard of this before in my life. It was arranged to see how hydrated the players were and how many of them were drinking what they shouldn't have been.

All you could see was a row of tubes full of urine, all with different colours. Some of them were clear, and others were dark yellow.

Eamonn gathered everyone in a circle, and pointed out the lads who he suspected were out the night before. They were told to f**k off and not come back! The lads walked off upset, and came back later on deeply apologetic for their exploits. They did extra training, and all was forgiven but it taught them a quick lesson.

Eamonn was only out to get the best out of everyone, and you had to s**t or got off the pot – or pass clear water in this case.

We reached the Ulster semi-finals in 2004 with Cavan, and would face Armagh in Clones after a superb 3-13 to 2-12 win over Down.

The Orchard were still in the All-Ireland conversation at this stage under Joe Kernan and still had the bulk of their 2002 side that went all the way. We made them really sweat but they just got past us, 0-13 to 0-11.

I stepped away from the Cavan camp in 2005, and sadly that's when Eamonn got sick, and was forced to step down as McElkennon took over.

Martin was well able to fill the void, but Eamonn's illness loomed large in the background and we all feared for him. Cavan were well beaten by Tyrone in the Ulster semi-finals and Mickey Harte's team went on to win their second All-Ireland.

I had also got involved with the Cavan minors, where Donal Keogan was in charge. We are still great friends to this day, and any team he is involved with he gets me in with him – including for his first season in a two-year stint as Cavan senior boss in 2007.

Down needed a replay to beat us in the Ulster Championship preliminary round in Newry, before Mayo ended our season in the backdoor when we couldn't handle Conor Mortimer, who scored 0-7.

WHEN EAMONN COLEMAN sadly passed away at the age of 59, the GAA world went into mourning when he died.

He was a fantastic man and it gives me great pleasure to say I got to work with him, but most importantly got to know him on a personal level.

His passing left a huge void in the GAA and he left his mark all over the country, and not just in Derry.

THE GOALKEEPING COACHING, and training teams, went on for a couple of years after that for me, and it brought me to St Osnat's in north Leitrim where we won a junior title.

I also had stints with Glenfarne-Kiltyclogher not far from Osnat's, as well as the Clonguish ladies' teams. At one stage, I was helping out goalkeepers at training all over the place.

I was loving life, until my world was turned upside down again in 2009.

And everything would change forever.

« CHAPTER 11 »

AT THE START of 2009, I was heading for 39 years of age, so the time to give up or throw in the towel in terms of playing football was approaching fast, but I didn't want to do that! So, I decided to do extra training, gym work and running just to get myself a bit of a jump-start and prolong things as much as I could.

I was in good shape, but I needed to stay that way because things could have gone by the wayside quickly otherwise.

One night after a good tough session on the field and in the gym, my legs were feeling sore and tender from the runs and other work I put myself through. I harmlessly ran my hand over my thigh and groin area to ease my weary legs, when I suddenly felt a lump. I didn't pay much heed to it, and like any typical man I thought no more of it and went on with life as normal.

Two or three weeks passed.

And I noticed it was still there, so I decided to see Dr Loftus – my old Leitrim team doctor who was familiar with my medical history and a man I really trusted.

We had a bit of a chat and he had a look, and he thought it might have been a thing called a Ganglion Cyst.

In plain English, this is basically a build-up of muscle or tissue, which would be no surprise from years of kicking a ball. Dr Loftus referred me to a specialist at Sligo University Hospital – which is a place I would become all too familiar with in a later chapter in life.

EIGHT MONTHS BEFORE all this, I also had a tumour in my jaw.

It was there for years. It wasn't giving me any pain so I didn't give it any heed, but it stuck out like a sore thumb.

For years my mother hounded me to get it checked, but I insisted it was okay because it wasn't giving me any real grief and I just presumed it was harmless. It was just me sweeping it to one side, brushing it under the carpet and hoping it would just go away. Like any Irish mammy, she kept worrying and like any Irish son I kept telling her it was alright – until I played in a club match around that time, and did a video interview afterwards.

When I watched it back, I sounded like a real bogger! I could really notice the tumour popping out every time I spoke.

Jaysus, that's big!

I hadn't realised how much it had grown, and I finally got off my arse to sort it out after watching that tape and hearing its impact as I spoke. I made an appointment to see Dr Marcus Choo at Sligo University Hospital, and he said it could be removed with an operation, but it would be severe.

It involved going at sinews and ligaments and all sorts of complicated stuff to take it out safely. He was confident it would be a success so I went ahead with it, and he said he would send the tumour off for a biopsy to check it for cancerous cells.

Surgery was no big deal to me. I had been there before but that dreaded 'cancer' word was cropping up and just like anyone else, I didn't like it.

That put the fear of God into me, but the procedure was successful and I was home again after five days in hospital – complete with 20 stitches on my jawline.

I looked like something from a Frankenstein movie, but the main thing was it was sorted and taken care of. Thankfully, a fortnight later my appointment for the biopsy results on the tumour was a happy one as it was deemed harmless, so there was no more said about it and I could get on with life once again.

I still have a small scar on my face from that procedure, but at least it's in line with my wrinkles so nobody ever seems to notice it!

But my experience from that did make me check things out a bit quicker than normal and to be a bit more vigilant. So I went to my appointment to see Dr Caldwell in Sligo. He had a look at the lump on my groin. He told me this would be a nice and simple procedure too, and I'd be home in a day or two with no hassle at all.

I had told my family about what was going to happen and that there was no panic. I went under the knife on a Friday afternoon to get the thing out of me. After around two hours I was out of the theatre, and I was kept overnight to recover because I was still a bit groggy.

Dr Caldwell also sent the lump away for analysis – the results were due back in a fortnight.

I WAS LIVING in Sligo at the time, having moved there in 2007 to work as a painter and decorator. Kilcawley Construction were sub-letting a lot of work to me, and things were all good.

Just four days after my operation on the Tuesday morning, I got a call from Dr Caldwell to come in for a chat because my results were back. On the drive up on that February afternoon in 2009, and in the lift up to level five in the building, I had no idea what he was about to tell me would change my life forever.

It was the first time I went to the doctor by myself, and the last time I went to the doctor by myself. I've told anyone I've met since then that if they are going for results, to bring somebody with them just to have someone there.

Little did I know what was to come. If I knew over the phone what was coming, I would have never gone alone or maybe not shown up at all. The word 'cancer' was never in my head, especially after the successful procedure on my jaw.

I thought it would be just like the last time, that the results would all be clear and I could go back to work in peace and move on. We both sat down, and he was directly in front of me when he said…

'Martin, I'm sorry to tell you this – but you have testicular cancer.'

I went into a daze straightaway and the room started to spin. The first thing that came into my head was death, but a whole range of emotions flooded through me. I went into a state of shock.

After around two minutes or so in utter disbelief, I asked him to repeat what he had said, because my mind was in overdrive. This was extremely difficult to process.

'Martin, I'm sorry to tell you this – but you have testicular cancer.'

THERE IT WAS again, but this time it came with a bit of reassurance.

In terms of how a cancer diagnosis goes, this was the best one to get because there was a high rate of success and, crucially, we had got to it early.

I had to go for an ultrasound on my testicles to see what was going on, so he said they'd be in touch when I was booked in for that later on in the afternoon.

I grabbed a cup of tea and the first phone call was to my mother, and I told her the news that no mam ever wants to hear – especially over the phone.

We both got upset, but once we gathered our thoughts together and spoke about it, she reassured me that I would have the support of my family and friends no matter what happened down the line.

Little did I know just how right she was. Knowing I wasn't going to be on my own helped my spirits a lot in that moment, because in Mr Caldwell's office I felt very isolated and scared.

But those assurances from my mother didn't suddenly cure me either. I had cancer. *What was going to happen to me? Was I going to die?* All of these awful questions spun around in my head a hundred times over in an awful mix of fear and dread.

I knew people who had been diagnosed with cancer before and within the space of a few months, they were dead and buried.

I got the shout for the ultrasound, and headed down to the area to get it done. I was asked to pull down my trousers and lie up on a table. My 'John Tom' was hanging to one side, and he didn't know what to do either!

They put gel all over my testicles like they do on a woman's tummy when she is having a baby scan, and off they went with the scan. I could see the screen with my testicles on it, and to my horror I could see there was a shadow on my left testicle… that was where the trouble was.

Dr Caldwell confirmed my worst fears, that there was a cancerous lump in that testicle… more bad news in such a short space of time. The next step was to see what could be done about it. Firstly, I was told the testicle had to be removed in Galway.

I went back to Dr Caldwell, and he referred me to Dr Sullivan at UCHG. I had an appointment to meet him within two weeks so we could plough on with the surgery. In the meantime, I went back to work to take my mind off things and what was ahead of me, but it didn't really help. Life was tough going.

Being sick with cancer and meeting my death was all I could think about. Nothing you can do takes your mind off it, even sleep.

The letter eventually arrived to see the specialist in UCHG, and on the morning of the appointment I was s****ting it because I had no idea what was coming. I really feared the worst as I found my way to Dr Sullivan's clinic.

This time, I brought my mother with me for support. My name was called and we both went in and chatted with the brilliant Dr Sullivan. He was an incredibly nice man, which helped me to stay calm. He asked me to lie up on the bed and pull down my pants, and he had a feel of what was going on downstairs.

It didn't bother me that he was having a root around, because it had to be done. It was done with dignity, but I can see how for some folk it can be a very uncomfortable and embarrassing experience – especially with their mother in the room.

After having a good feel and locating the lump, he told me that the testicle had to come out, which was no surprise and, in another fortnight, I was to return to get my bloods taken, have another ultrasound scan and an MRI to get a better picture of what we were facing.

In all of this time I was incredibly calm, maybe because things seemed to be moving very quickly. That was probably all down to the seriousness of the situation. It is amazing how brave you can become when this sort of situation actually happens.

At my next appointment in Galway, Dr Sullivan came back in after the MRI and the scans and had four student doctors with him – two males and two females.

He asked me if I wouldn't mind if his trainees could examine the lump on my testicle, and I agreed. The trousers came down again.

I lay down, and the students were given a quick brief on my story. The two male student doctors proceeded to have a feel, and that was it.

But the two females were next, and I had to beg myself inside my head to stay in control… not to get too excited, if you know what I mean. This was a time for calm if ever there was one!

Their soft warm hands started to feel me up, but thankfully I managed to stay in control without any awkward moments and I pulled my trousers back up as quickly as possible when they were finished.

But in all seriousness, the whole process of being examined like that was terrifying. It had to be done, however. I had to wait for my next appointment to discuss the procedure.

I was home one weekend, where my brothers Pete, Leo and JJ were all there along with my sister Marian and we were all chatting things over.

We had a bit of a banter and a laugh when we spoke about my illness; it was all light-hearted. Marian said that cancer only hits one in four, so she thanked me for taking the hit in our family.

We all burst out laughing, and even mammy eventually started laughing with us too. JJ told me it was typical that that's what I got for never having a drink too.

But it was funny, because I had been an elite sportsman for most of my life. I never drank and never really smoked, bar that time daddy caught us and we nipped it in the bud all those years ago.

When I was diagnosed, I had all these questions as to why I got it at the age of 39 given I was in fairly good health and had no bad habits. That was going through my mind all the time.

Why me?

What did I do wrong to deserve this sort of punishment?

WHEN I WAS by myself, I thought about nothing but death when it came to what I was facing. But talking about it at home and having a bit of banter about it with my family really lightened the mood and helped me deal with it all.

It's horrible to hear those three words… 'You have cancer,' but there's two ways you can go with it.

You can take it head on and accept it and fight it.

Or go into the corner and feel sorry for yourself and let it get to you… and it will beat you if you let it win.

I had so many battles on the field of play, but this was going to be my biggest by a mile and talking and being humorous about it was a massive help. It's a bit of an Irish thing, and it certainly worked for me and my loved ones.

I had received an appointment to discuss the next step and removing the testicle. I thought they were just going to open my sack literally like a bag, take out the testicle like a little ball and I'd go home, but it was a lot more complicated than that!

They had to make an incision just above my groin, move down through my leg and take out the testicle and the tube that comes with it.

It was daunting to say the least, but I accepted how it was going to happen because I had no choice.

NEXT UP WAS to tell my teammates in Clonguish the news. We were all in a circle at training one night, and I broke the ice and told them about my ordeal and what I was facing in the coming weeks and months.

Training went on, and the lads being the lads started taking the piss. We had a good training hard session but it was filled with a lot of laughs to lighten the mood. It really helped me a lot that I wasn't going to be mollycoddled by the boys and a bit of a sympathy case around the club.

The news was out now, and I was getting phone calls every few days from family and friends wishing me the best, which was a big thing too, because now I really felt like I wasn't on my own.

It was fight or take flight, and having all of that support was half the battle the whole way through things. The operation was down for a Monday in April, so I finished up a few small jobs on the Friday afternoon beforehand.

The hospital in Galway called me up to be admitted on the Friday night, so I could be all set and first in on the Monday morning to have my testicle taken out and, to me, I could have a nice relaxing couple of days in there before the operation.

But we had a league match with Clonguish against Ballymahon on the Sunday afternoon, and as serious as this all was, I didn't want to miss it. The GAA was my oxygen and I needed to play.

I had no idea what was in store for me after this, so I was determined to make that match while I was still fit and strong. Some quick thinking kicked in, and I said to them I'd need to go into town for a while on the Sunday to grab a few essentials like pyjamas, magazines and toiletries as I'd be in hospital for at least a week.

They gave me the green light, as long as I cleared it with the nurses on the ward. So, I packed a bag for the hospital with pyjamas and all that craic already in it… as well as my gear for the match.

I drove down on the Friday evening, got my bed and on Sunday morning I had to make my way to Ballymahon to play the game, and it's a good hour and a half of a drive from Galway city.

The nurses gave me the all clear to go and do my 'shopping,' so I hopped in the car and off I went.

WHEN I ARRIVED, I felt bad about playing – not because I had pulled a fast one on the nurses, but because I knew my year was pretty much over. So Stephen

Watters rightfully went in goal and I sat on the bench.

We were losing at half-time, and I was summoned to the goals, so Stephen could go midfield, because he was a big man and we were being cleaned out there. We ended up winning, and it was a nice way to sign off before I went into the unknown. I wished the lads the best of luck for the rest of the year, and I got a bit emotional as I said my farewells.

This was the first time I was about to say goodbye to the game for a lengthy period, and possibly forever.

The GAA was a lifelong part of me. I played in muck and dirt on wet January nights and on the dry summer sod year in and year out, and I was so determined that cancer was not going to stop that.

I eventually got back to Galway without knowing if and when I would ever be in that dressing-room again. Thankfully, the nurses never copped on that I was gone for an age and had travelled across the country to play a game.

I came back with no shopping with me at all and I quickly hopped back into the bed, happy out with my genius little masterstroke before the really serious business the following day.

« CHAPTER 12 »

I WOKE UP on the Monday morning and they kitted me out in my blue gown, the silly blue hat and these special knickers you have to wear when they're taking away one of your testicles.

I was called down for surgery and put on a trolley and wheeled into theatre and the nerves kicked in a little. It is daunting, but I didn't let it bother me too much.

There were questions galore when I got to the theatre and was under those lights, as I confirmed my name and date of birth and it was explained, one last time, what was about to happen.

I trusted the process and was all set to be knocked out… and they told me to count back from 10. Being the stubborn man I am, I always tried to get as far as one… but that never happens! *10, nine… eight… gone…* lights out!

I woke up a while later and I was totally away with the birds.

'Martin, Martin! We need to slide you onto the bed!'

I was all over the shop, and I was numb from the waist down.

I started screaming, 'My legs! I can't feel my legs! Let me do a few f***in' stretches!'

The nurse started laughing and told me to work away at the stretches, and I was just sliding over and back in the bed like a raving eejit.

When I came around fully, they took my blood pressure and gave me a vital cup of tea with some toast. And it dawned on me that the surgery was over.

Naturally enough, it also dawned on me what I had just been through and I slid my hand downstairs, really slowly, to see if they really had taken one of my balls – and, sure enough, junior was on his own down there!

It was such a strange feeling waking up with one testicle. I did have the option of a prosthetic ball to fill the gap to make it feel as if I had both, but I didn't bother with it.

I stayed in hospital for the rest of the week, and after some more recovery I eventually went back to work at the painting because I needed money coming in at the same time.

But the scans in Galway kept coming as the doctors weighed up the best plan of action in terms of treatment, because there were three options.

I could have radiotherapy, chemotherapy… or both.

Then it was time for a Pet Scan, which is the one to get as it checks every part of your body, and they came to the conclusion that my initial lump in my groin should have been found in my stomach.

My case file was sent to England to try and get to the bottom of that, and they concluded that I must have got hurt in my scrotum years ago from a kick or a bang playing football, or something else.

Cancer travels in small blood vessels and a minor incision meant that the vein was blocked, so in a mad stroke of luck, the cancer stopped there.

It's like blocking a stream, but it saved me from even more serious damage. Had it made its way through, it should have reached my vital organs and that would have been totally catastrophic.

Just to make sure they reached any possible cancer elsewhere in my body, chemotherapy treatment was the way to go to flush me out, so we went with that.

I WAS STILL in constant contact with the family and the lads from football. But little did I know the s**t was going to hit the fan come June when the treatment started.

It all had to be done in UCHG, and I had to stay there so they could keep an eye on me. The treatment was going to be very intense, so they initially decided to give me three sessions of it.

I was to get a dose of chemo on a Monday, Tuesday, Wednesday, Thursday, and Friday… and back at it the following Thursday again. I would then have a week off, and had to go back in again the following Thursday after that, which was all one cycle.

It was relentless for five or six hours a day, and I had to get through three bags of it per day too. Don't ask me the name of the stuff, but the drugs drip into your bloodstream at a controlled rate using an IV bag.

The intensity was to make sure they killed every cancerous cell in my body, and they give you this horror list of what happens to you in terms of losing weight, putting on weight, losing your hair, your appetite going, mouth ulcers, diarrhoea… you name it.

It looked like I was about to go to hell and back, but reading it on a page and actually going through it are two totally different things.

I went to Galway on the Sunday night to get started.

I was in a ward with six other cancer patients. Some were older than me, and some were younger and they all had different types of cancer.

When I was due to start, the nurse came in with an apron and gloves on and a whole tray of tablets and injections.

'Here we go!'

I lay down – the tablets were for anti-sickness – and the injection went into my drip. Then I got a serious itch on my arse, and thought I was getting piles. *Wasn't this just typical, on top of everything else?*

She had me all hooked up and the pump was running, and I didn't know what to expect. *Is this going to hurt me? Will it burn my arm? Is this going to be very uncomfortable?*

But when it was motoring, it was like a normal drip going into the arm and I didn't feel anything, much to my relief. It went on for the whole day, and I just chilled out and watched a bit of telly and read some magazines. When I was done, I had a shower and some food and I felt great.

Morning two was the same routine – nurse, tray, tablet, injections – and the itchy arse. The nurse noticed my discomfort and asked me what was wrong, but she said it was a side effect of the anti-sickness drug… they called it 'ants in the pants'. I was just glad it was all normal in these circumstances, and that I didn't have piles.

It went on like that every day, and at the end of the week they told me they'd see me again in a fortnight, and I had to do two chemo sessions in Sligo in between.

I FELT GOOD. I packed up and drove home into the lovely evening and relaxed when I got back to the house, wondering what all the fuss was about.

The weather was lovely on the Saturday morning, so I said I'd go out and mow the lawn but five minutes into it, I started puking my guts up. I suddenly felt exhausted, and kept getting sick.

This was the real start of it.

So, I had to take it easy and listen to my body. I was tired a lot, and I got through another two x two-hour sessions in Sligo before a week off... and back to Galway again for the next bout.

My hair was still there, but I was knackered constantly.

When it was time to go back for the big sessions at UCHG and I went for a shower after the first session, lumps of hair started streaming off my head.

I decided to shave it off there and then, and I didn't even really need any shaving foam because most of it just fell out of my head and onto the floor.

It was time to prepare for the worst and hope for the best, and suddenly here was this bald man looking back at me in the mirror.

I knew the hair was going to go at some stage, and when it did it unveiled a big scar at the side of my head from a kick on the football pitch, and another at the back where a trailer hit the side of my head as I loaded sticks on it years ago.

These battle wounds made me laugh in front of that mirror. I looked like a real rough buff who just came in from the scrap of his life... but he was ready for this one too. When I came back into the room, four of the other six patients were bald too, so this was the norm. And that eased me into accepting the hair loss. We were all told it would come back down the line.

I found myself getting more and more tired as the sessions went on, and my appetite was going completely out the door.

They brought us stew one day for dinner, which I love, but when I saw it on the plate I ran to the toilet and got violently sick. All I was able for was a small bit of jelly and ice cream, and I somehow managed to get that into me.

Across from UCHG is a Supermac's on the Newcastle Road. Anyone who has visited that hospital is probably familiar with it.

After one chemo session I had a mad craving for a burger, so I went and got one. The trick was to eat small, but I found myself in that Supermac's most evenings for a little treat.

My aunt Jackie lived in Galway and she was great for popping in to see me regularly and keeping my spirits up, so I never felt I was on my own with her close by. Sadly, she has since passed away from cancer herself. But the third block of chemo really took it out of me. After that week I was extremely sick and beyond exhausted, and my personality really began to change.

My emotions were all over the place.

I didn't want anybody near me, and just wanted to be by myself. I was waking up at four or five in the morning craving hot chocolate and toast, which was a bit mad.

I'd go back to bed until noon, get up and manage to have some food and go back to sleep again. I could barely function, and it was really hitting home that this was all coming to a head and the treatment was really taking it out of me.

At my lowest point, I was puking and had diarrhoea at the same time. Nobody needs to imagine me sitting on a toilet going from both ends. That lasted three or four days. I felt like I couldn't take the pain any more, and at that stage I just wanted God to take me. I could just see no way out, and what my body was going through was just too much for me to handle.

I was tired, was constantly sick, and killed with diarrhoea. I had mood swings, and everything was going against me. I could see no hope, could see no way out. I just wanted to leave this life, because the pain was too much.

This was rock bottom, and it went on for a few hours as I grappled with my thoughts… but just wanted death to come and put me out of my misery.

But in the midst of it all, the phone rang.

IT WAS FROM a man at a club in Cavan called Killinaleck. I had helped them the year before with a few training sessions and worked with their goalkeepers.

I told him things weren't good at the moment, but I asked him what he wanted? He knew I was in a bad place but he was honest with me and said he was calling to see if I could come to one of their training sessions that night.

He realised how low I was and said he was sorry he called, and he hoped I would feel better soon.

'I'll go!' I barked back.

I told him I'd be there a half an hour before the session! So I went for a nap, and all of a sudden a new energy came over me as I went and got my gear together.

This is what would keep me alive.

I was like a new man as I went around the place looking for gear and boots and all of my other bits and pieces.

I was never going to be pushing it, but suddenly I wasn't thinking about diarrhoea, puking, losing my hair, having one testicle or wanting to die. When I arrived at the pitch, I secretly puked a little before we got started. I washed out my mouth and got myself together, and the manager introduced me to the panel.

They all told me I was looking well, despite the baldness and the fact that I was clearly visibly shook – but I gave them a training session as best I could, and did a bit with the 'keepers too.

When I walked out to the field first, I realised that this is where I wanted to be, and where I needed to be. Football would be my cure.

Any GAA pitch is a field of dreams in my eyes.

It's where I belong. After the session I drove home a happy man, and spewed my guts up. I knew I over-did it, but I just couldn't help it.

But from that moment, I knew I had to get back to football and stay involved – just to get out of the house if anything. It would give me a purpose, and a vital one at that.

On that Saturday evening I went down to see my Clonguish teammates – I arrived around 20 minutes before they started training.

Some lads were on the field already, and the slagging started straight away. 'Ah McHugh... ya fat-arse! Great to see ya!' Enda Williams came out and gave my head a little shine. They were all delighted to see me.

The shouting kept going all through the session, and one of the lads called John Dowd was hovering around the middle of the field. He's a giant of a man, and well over six feet tall. He was a strong player but was as awkward as two left feet, and was liable to say anything to anyone. In the middle of the session, he found a sliotar and roared... 'Hey, McHugh! Is that your ball?!'

Some of the lads didn't know where to look because they probably thought the comment was sailing a bit close to the wind.

But I started laughing away, and sharply replied, 'No, sure didn't I lose mine humping your Mrs last night!'

The lads all erupted with laughter. I might have been bald and sick, but the wit and being able to slag was still there and those weapons are as vital as any in a football panel.

The lads were going through a bit of a sticky patch around that time, and attitudes were not where they should have been. That's when Liam Doherty, the coach, asked me over to say a few words to them.

I WONDERED WHAT I would come out with, and then it hit me.

I gathered the lads around in a circle and asked Paddy Dowd to kick a ball over to me. With that, I tried to kick it back to him but I just couldn't.

The lads had gone from being astounded at how long I could kick the ball to watching me only send it a yard or two. I had no power left in my legs at all, and that's where my rant began.

'I'm not able to kick the ball anymore lads, and you are all crying and giving excuses when it comes to training and performing at your best. Look at me, I'm actually dying.

'I'm not able to play, and that's killing me.

'I'm not even able to train or kick the ball, and that's killing me.

'And you are all whinging and crying?'

I told them I'd come to support them at every game they played, even if I had to bring the bed with me.

I told them this could be another huge chance for them to win a championship, and begged them not to leave it behind them.

When I stopped, they all clapped.

I hoped my words gave them a new perspective on things, and I think they did.

True to my word, I got to their matches, and they got to the county final against Dromard.

In the last training session, the Friday before the game, I decided to tog out and do a little warm-up. I went off to do a lap, but halfway through it I just had to stop and walk back.

I had absolutely nothing left in me and had to stay in my lane, but I was still there for the game, which finished in a draw at 1-11 each.

Come the replay, we were all in the dressing-room and I told the goalkeeper, Stephen, if we were well ahead with a few minutes left to fake an injury so I could come on, and I'd retire a happy man. He agreed, but at half-time the match was level and the lads were shocking beyond belief. When we regrouped in the Pearse Park dressing-room the blame game started.

Fingers were being pointed regarding the poor performance. Nobody was taking any responsibility, and the atmosphere in the room was toxic.

The management were outside the room in the corridor having their discussion, as the players were barking and ripping each other to pieces inside.

I just couldn't take it anymore.

I stood up and lit the roof with my language. 'What the f**k is going on lads!! Why are we playing shite??

'I want to be out there but I can't, and I don't need to remind you all right now I'm dying. Cop the f**k on!'

The room fell silent and I kept going. 'There are 30 people in this dressing-room, 30 in the other, and 3,000 people in the stand. Nobody here can tell me that they will be HERE again next year!'

I told them they needed the game of their lives if they wanted that first title in five years. Nobody was to come back in again in half an hour as a loser.

The management said nothing because there was nothing left to be said. We won the game by a point.

I was out on the field congratulating all the lads when the legendary Paul Barden grabbed me and told me to come and lift the cup with him.

He is an all-time Longford icon and the hero on the day, because his pointed free in stoppage time sealed a 0-9 to 1-5 victory.

I insisted I couldn't possibly lift the cup, because this was their day. But he was adamant I did, given the speech I made at half-time and how my presence had helped drive them on a bit to get the job done.

I only had an old hoodie on me, but someone threw me a jersey and I put it on. I looked down at all the supporters.

And myself and Paul lifted the cup to absolutely joyous scenes.

That was a huge moment for me, because I felt part of a group of lads who had fought tooth and nail and did whatever it took to win.

I got a medal and all, and I'd rate it as my number one. Because in that moment there and then with the cup over my head, I knew I had beaten cancer.

PART **FIVE**

Lightning Strikes Twice

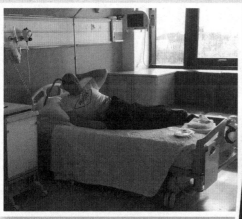

I fought cancer and won twice, and I'm always prepared to keep on that fight if I have to! Here I am (above) back in a hospital bed after 'lightning did strike twice'. I would not have been able to defeat it on my own. Without football in all its guises I don't know what would have happened, but moments like moving back to Aughnasheelin and getting to win the county intermediate title with my home club in 2017 (right) make you want to live and play the game forever. However, football only helps so much, and without the love and support of my partner Linda I do not know where I would be today.

« CHAPTER 13 »

THE CELEBRATIONS AFTER winning that title were great, but they didn't last long for me because, inevitably, I got very tired.

It was a huge turning point for me, but at the same time the whole experience just took so much out of me physically and mentally. When the party was getting started that night, I was at home conked out in bed!

I was like that for a long time. Because the intensity of the treatment really took it out of me and it took months for my body to return to functioning close to normal again.

I was always exhausted.

But something magical was happening in the background, and I hadn't a clue about it. Clonguish had organised a fundraiser for me in the form of a function, and I found out about it on the day we won the final.

That kindness from others brought a tear to my eye, because I never envisaged this. A few weeks passed, and it took place in the Shannon Key West Hotel in Rooskey that October.

A few people were there and the band was warming-up as I arrived. I was welcomed by my mother and brother. Within a half an hour, the place was packed. There were friends and neighbours from back home, and people there from counties all over the place after my involvement with so many football teams down through the years.

They were all there as a mark of support and appreciation for what I'd been through, and I was absolutely gob-smacked.

I GOT UP to make a speech and was just totally overwhelmed with emotion. I looked across the packed room. There were nearly 400 people there to support me.

It was really special and incredibly humbling, because my home club Aughnasheelin got on board to help and organise it too.

It just meant so much to me, and I am still eternally grateful for that gesture and all the work that went into organising it.

Work just wasn't an option during that period because I was so fatigued, but bills were coming in and rent had to be paid. When that winter kicked in, I didn't really do much, because I still wasn't able, so the fundraiser was a huge help when it came to keeping the wolf from the door.

On top of that, seeing all of those people coming out in support really kept me going during those dark days when the evenings got shorter.

By the time 2010 rolled around, I felt a bit stronger and eventually went back to do a bit of training with Clonguish. It took a good few months of that before I got back to one hundred percent, and during that season I never got fully back to my best. But for a man heading into his 40th year, that still wasn't bad going and I was just delighted to be putting on the gloves again. It kept me out of the house, gave me something to aim for and I gradually built my strength up again naturally.

People were offering me remedies and a few quick solutions to make my body heal and recover a bit quicker, but I wanted it all to happen naturally and not push myself too hard.

Enough had gone through my system already, and letting my body do its own thing sort of worked, because I did get the odd run in goals when Stephen Watters was hurt or not around. Because of my age, I was still able to play at a lower standard even though I lined out for the senior team from time to time. That took a bit of the pressure off me and sustained my interest.

We were able to field three teams because we had so many players, and in that campaign I played plenty of Division 2 football.

Again, it just meant so much to me to be involved. Getting out of the house to go to training, coach a team, or even see my teammates meant the world to me and gave me a real purpose and a reason to get out of bed.

Even though I still wasn't able to go back to work, it was vital that I had something to do for both mind and body. Football always provided that.

THE GAA SAVED my life over those years, one hundred percent and without a shadow of doubt. Otherwise, I had nothing to get out of bed for!

It was huge progress from miserably sitting on the toilet, my throat red raw from puking and having diarrhoea and just wanting to leave this world as my body constantly attacked me.

Getting that phone call from Cavan helped me see the light again, and my life slowly rebuilt from there. At this point, I knew I had to sustain that to stay going. I still had a lot of free time, so I took up fishing as a hobby too and I still love it. It's great being outdoors in the fresh air and I find it incredibly relaxing.

Weeks on end indoors would have meant the end for me in terms of sport for sure – whether it was GAA or soccer or anything at all, it was imperative that I got outside as much as I could.

Getting off my arse helped me turn that corner, and laid the platform for new departures in life after that. I just didn't know it at the time.

Social welfare and illness benefits also kept the wolf from the door financially, and I was entitled to rent allowance as well which proved to be a huge help. I got a medical card not long after I got sick too, and it was vital because I had to take anti-sickness tablets for months after my treatment finished. And it helped with all the other medical bills too.

I could find myself getting stronger, but a full day's work was still beyond me, though I would do odd jobs here and there around my own house or for my mother. She wanted me to paint a fence outside her house, but it was around 40 metres long… front and back. Usually, it would have taken me two hours, but it took me nearly six… and I had to take a break in the middle for a nap.

That was an eye-opener, because it made me realise I wasn't ready to start looking for proper work again and get back on my feet.

TURNING 40 CAME and went, and even thought I was still so weak, I had a totally different perspective on life.

My whole outlook before cancer and after cancer was like chalk and cheese. The old me was working his arse to the bone and working a lot of weekends.

I was always trying to keep Tom, Dick and Harry happy. I was always swimming against the tide and burning the candle at both ends, and I never really stopped to think about looking after myself.

When I was lying in that bed and extremely ill from the third chemo session, I started looking back on how I was living and thought... *What the f**k was I doing?*

I never once took time out to look after myself, chill out or just go for a night away and have a bit of craic or just switch off. Football was always there for me and as much as I loved it, it papered over a lot of cracks in my life. I had no idea, but I hadn't been looking after myself at all.

When football was over every year, I was straight back on the hamster wheel the next morning with work and trying to bite off more than I could chew and it proved to be a big hindrance.

I was taking on too much with the painting work, and constantly driving from 'A' to 'B' to keep it all moving. I should have stayed in my lane, and only accepted what was manageable. I put myself under undue pressure, and it could not have helped when it came to getting seriously sick.

But when the hard times arrived, football saved me. It clicked that I needed to embrace the game and enjoy it again, and just chill out a bit more and look after number one. It helped me enjoy life more as a whole. I had more of a laugh. I stopped panicking about stupid stuff... it was a big game-changer.

Before I got sick, I had been such a goody-two-shoes. I never drank and never got arrested or anything like that, and after coming out the other side of it, I said I'd go daft and get a tattoo.

I got Chinese writing across my left arm that translates as 'warrior,' because up in Clonguish the lads used to call me that.

Then in 2010 I got one on my other arm of a big Asian design. I literally closed my eyes and picked it out of a book just for the craic of it... and it stretches from my shoulder to my forearm.

2011 came and went and I was still taking life at a slow pace, easing myself in when it came to sport and gradually building myself up in terms of strength as the illness faded and my hair started to appear back on my head.

I had to go back to get bloods done and have checks every few weeks, and the doctors constantly warned me not to push myself. The body needed loads of time to heal naturally, and I had to be patient.

Before I knew it, it was 2013 and time to start another campaign with Clonguish. The years were really rolling by… I was 42, heading on 43 at this stage.

I was getting older and slower, but my mindset was still great. I knew my level, so I concentrated on the second and third teams when I went back because I knew the senior team was just out of reach.

Training was more intense at senior level at that stage, and it was no harm taking a bit of a back seat and providing cover for the first team when they needed it.

Retirement was in sight really, because I won all I could have won and I could find my health getting fully back to normal.

AS THAT YEAR rolled on, I felt I was missing something. I didn't want to be sitting on my arse doing nothing, but I was still too sick to return to employment.

A friend suggested going to the Vocational Education Committee about doing a course, so I said I would have a look and see what was on offer. I hadn't a clue what to do, but I had nothing to lose.

Because I was sick it was going to cost me nothing either, and they gave me a list of 40 odd courses to do. Me and school never combined well, and I'll not shy away from the fact that I'm not the sharpest tool in the box.

When I walked out of the classroom at 16, I thought that was it for me in terms of education, and was content enough to say goodbye to the books forever… *Good luck… I'm finished!'*

I was referred to a guidance counsellor, filled in my details about my sickness and how young I was when I left school, and she suggested doing a level three course to see how I got on, because it wouldn't be too difficult. I could use it as a platform to build on and see where I was at.

That helped me a lot to make the right choice and cut my cloth to measure. It was important to start off slow and easy, and it was definitely the way to go because I would have quit after two months had I started off with a more difficult course.

I had been away from education for so long, so I had to ease myself back in. It would only be two classes a week, and I spotted one on Computers and Healthcare. I had no idea what was ahead of me, but I said I'd do it because it was free and it was just something to get me out of the house too.

The course was great, and it gave me a big boost of confidence when I realised I was more able for it than some of the others in the room.

My healthcare tutor was Ann Gallagher. She taught us well but always picked on the Leitrim man. There were 20 of us in the class at the start, but as the weeks and months went on there were only eight of us left as my classmates dropped like flies.

I was really enjoying it, and I developed a sudden interest in healthcare as a result. Even though this was only level three and was quite simple, it was capturing my attention – and it gave me even more purpose in life because I was genuinely interested.

Some days I might have a class during the day and training in the evening, and I would be exhausted after it all. But it didn't stop me helping out other clubs as a coach, like St Osnat's Glencar in north Leitrim.

They were a typical junior team that were training in a field beside a river, with just two footballs and maybe nine or 10 lads. I came up for a session and brought a few footballs with me, and between the first session and the third one, we managed to gather an extra 20 players.

On the field, we won the league and the Leader Cup with Clonguish, but I was still cautious not to overdo things in terms of football so I didn't burn out. However, between helping to train teams, playing a bit of soccer with Ballygawley Celtic and the course, I had plenty to keep me occupied and it was great.

The soccer was great craic on Sunday mornings, and it was often too much craic. Some of the lads would turn up half cut from the night before or even came to the games straight from the pub on the rollover!

The manager would be ringing lads 10 minutes before kick-off asking them where they were, which was half the craic of it all. It wasn't too serious and totally different to GAA, but that was the beauty of it. It was time for me to just enjoy it all now, have a bit of a laugh and relish whatever time I had left as a player.

THE SOCIAL WELFARE benefits were keeping me above water in terms of money, and I was getting stronger and was able to do more work around the house.

But I was still getting tired in the evenings – three years on from the chemo, and I'm sure a lot of that was down to getting older too. At the end of that year, I was into really unfamiliar territory, because I had exams and assignments to do.

I was cruising through it though, and coming back with As and Bs. I had never seen those grades on top of a sheet before, so it was a nice boost.

By now I was playing soccer with a club called Merville United in Sligo town beside the Showgrounds where Sligo Rovers play, and it was a decent way to pass another winter and keep myself in shape without busting a gut.

Having two years taken away when you are too weak to train made me really hate being unfit, so I joined a gym in Ballisodare as well, where I was now living to keep myself in check.

Through 2014 I hadn't been playing too much senior football with Clonguish and was heading for 44. I had won plenty with them and loved being around the club, but I still pondered retiring. But at the start of 2015 the football bug came back, and I could hear Aughnasheelin calling in the back of my mind.

This was where I was from, where I grew up and where it all started when I was 10 years old – and I felt like this was where it should finish. I had this strange feeling that there was more in me, but not with Clonguish and maybe it was time to move on from there.

There was travelling involved to train and play with them now since the move to Ballisodare in Sligo; it was senior football and my body wasn't able for that level of training any more. Or so I thought.

Eventually, the papers were signed to go back to my home club, and I was welcomed back with open arms. My first match back was a junior game against Kiltubrid, and I was a sub.

I didn't mind being on the bench at all, but we were losing at half-time and I was told to get on the field to go in goals. I warmed-up and we ended up winning, and that feeling was back again. Here I was, back between the sticks in the green and white of Aughnasheelin.

We got to the semi-final of the championship, and the football spark that was fading a bit with Clonguish was suddenly back with a bang in my home colours.

Meanwhile, as we were finishing up with the healthcare course, the tutor began telling us about the next steps if we wanted to take them.

TO GET A job with the HSE you needed a level five healthcare qualification, which would mean another course, which would be a bit more intense.

But a job with the HSE would mean security, good money and double-time on a Sunday. She had my ear with all of that (especially the double-time on a Sunday!) and it really got me thinking.

The level five course was worth a go at least, just to see how I got on. Again, I had absolutely nothing to lose and had passed this one with flying colours. It was two classes a week again, but they were longer and ran from 9.30am until 2.30pm, but I went for it because I didn't want to have any regrets and I had an ambition to take things a step further.

It certainly was more intense, because nearly every second or third week an assignment was due, and there was a lot involved. We had to learn about the anatomy of the body, dealing with patients and handling all sorts of different scenarios that can unfold in a healthcare environment.

We were taught about minding the elderly, dementia patients and caring for all sorts of people with every kind of illness imaginable. There was no hands-on work with actual patients, but we were shown a lot of videos and slides and given a lot of verbal instruction about working in a hospital environment as we went along.

It was a lot to take on and I thought some of it was a complete waste of time, because I remember having to learn about how the lungs and intestines and liver all function, but we weren't training to be surgeons either.

We had over a dozen practical classes and every one of those had an exam at the end.

There was work experience too and in the middle of the second semester, I had an eye on Sligo University Hospital to get my foot in the door there, because if I did get employment down the line it would be the ideal place for me.

A nursing home would have been another option but it is very labour intensive, hoisting people in and out of beds all day and I didn't want to be pinned down in one small facility like that.

The hospital was more expansive with seven or eight floors of wards, and I just knew it would throw something different at me every day. I just preferred the thought of that.

But the course wasn't over yet, and the assignments were coming thick and fast, but I was more prepared for the workload with the level three course under my belt, and most importantly I was able to keep my head above water.

WHEN IT GOT heavy near the end, I was able to do it. Between football and going back to education, life was really good again but I was starting to miss being a working man and having a proper wage at the end of the week. The course was my gateway to achieving that.

I had survived from week-to-week, but I was getting sick of money being tight. When I moved to Ballisodare, I lost my rent allowance so any wiggle room I had was pretty much gone and being short of cash at my age was really frustrating.

The bills were coming thick and fast, and my landlord wouldn't drop the rent so I had to move somewhere with cheaper rent in order to get my rent allowance back and give myself some badly needed breathing space. Eventually, I got a lovely farmhouse out in the countryside in the village of Ballygawley, south of Sligo town.

The place was only €450 a month and I got the rent allowance back, which was a massive help. I was delighted with my new digs.

Suddenly, I was able to make ends meet again, but still had to watch every penny at the same time. Any time I was short of money, thankfully I was able to ask my family for help instead of the banks, and they never let me down.

It's embarrassing to be short of money and have to put the begging bowl out, but I was often left with no choice as I had been out of work for so long. The time for work experience eventually rolled around; we had to put in some paperwork and I got what I was looking for and would do it at Sligo University Hospital.

All of my work in those courses was going to boil down to how I performed in the hospital – no more than putting in endless nights of training for the championship. I had to see for myself if this was what I really wanted to do as well, because you can do all the classes in the world but nothing prepares you for doing the real thing and it coming at you every day.

I met all the bosses and I was sent to the short stay unit in the hospital. The lady in charge of the ward, I was told on the quiet, was a bit bossy, very strict and by the book, so she wouldn't take any messing.

This wasn't a great start as far as I was concerned, but another healthcare assistant called Patricia was going to be my guide for the day to show me the ropes and help me to settle in.

Helping her with the patients was also part of my brief, so we went into one fella and we had to sit him up for his breakfast. We'll just call him Paddy... but poor Paddy had dementia.

'Hi Paddy... I'm Martin, I'm going to give you a hand with your breakfast.' In plain English, Paddy told me to f**k off.

At that point I didn't know where to look because Patricia was standing there, and this was the first of many examples of something we hadn't been taught about in the classes on the course!

Patricia was well used to this, and reassured me that a lot of the dementia patients do not know what they are at or even who they are. That's just the sad reality of it, but thankfully Paddy eventually had his breakfast after his tirade against me and we left him at it.

We went to the next room and Paddy number two was waiting for us, but he had gone to the toilet everywhere. It was all down his leg, up his back and everywhere else bar the toilet. That was another class I must have missed, because we had to clean him up.

My stomach was starting to turn, and I was already questioning my life choices with the course and the placement at the hospital. Patricia reassured me that I'd get used to it, and sure enough as the days went on things got a bit easier and I got to grips with what the gig entailed.

The shock factor wasn't long going away and I soon got used to different types of patients and their personalities, and I started to like it.

Then, I found myself really enjoying it, and I worked really well with all of the patients regardless of what was wrong with them. I engaged with them as much as I could in a light-hearted way to put them and myself at ease, and by and large it worked.

Even the strict C&M – which stands for certified nurse and midwife – was very impressed at how I dealt with the patients and handled myself in general.

The patients were really responding to me, and that was hugely positive.

IN THE LAST three or four shifts of the second week with the placement drawing to a close, I asked Patricia how to get in and get a job with the HSE.

Forms had to be filled out and you had to wait for a call, but that sounded like a real stab in the dark. Another option was you could contact TTM Ireland – a healthcare recruitment agency based in Ennis who provided healthcare staff for the HSE directly.

The next step was to just ring them up. I explained that I was on work placement in Sligo and had nearly finished my level five qualification in Healthcare. I had to send plenty of paperwork and forms into them, and when my work experience was finished I had to get my workbook signed by the C&M and my tutor.

Thankfully, my tutor gave me an 'A' with a glowing reference which was a huge help, and I sent the whole lot off to them.

It took me no time to gather everything up and send it off along with details of the vaccines I had taken against various illnesses, a letter from my GP to say I was healthy, and an up-to-date Garda vetting form.

On a Friday afternoon that August, I went to the doctor to finally get the all-clear to work after my battle with cancer and my long journey back to full strength from the chemotherapy and everything else my body had gone through.

I had my bloods taken every three months to keep things in check. For the first year after my illness I went for a scan every six months just to make sure everything was above board and all clear.

From 2009 until '15, by the time I finished the level five course, everything was great. I had furthered my education, found my love for football again and was about to start an exciting new career.

But just as I was about to get my all-healthy letter, the doctor looked through some blood results.

My kidney and liver were both okay, but my cholesterol was up which was no surprise – as I was a bit on the fat side at this stage and tended to enjoy myself at the dinner table. But my PSA was up too – which was related to my prostate. When the doctor told me that, I had no idea what either of those were!

According to Google, your PSA is the Prostate-specific antigen, which is a protein produced by normal, as well as malignant, cells of the prostate gland and it all sounds like very complicated stuff, especially when you hear it for the first time.

It was only up slightly at 2.2, but I was given a fit to work letter anyway and with that, I was in with TTM recruitment, and before long I was officially a healthcare assistant.

But because of my recent medical history they wanted me to do another blood test, just to be sure. There is never any harm in double-checking. And my PSA was up again… this time to 3.4.

I still didn't realise what was happening and didn't pay any real heed to it, but I was told I had to attend the rapid prostate unit in my old haunt of Galway University Hospital and get more blood tests done in the meantime.

I had no inclination that something major could be on the cards, especially as I was after winning one hell of a battle already. I was happy out with my new life as a care assistant in Sligo General and, for the first time in years, I just loved what I was doing.

BY OCTOBER, IT was time to visit the rapid prostate unit and the PSA was up even further to 5.4, which was more than double the original figure, so alarm bells had started to ring. The doctor there decided to do a quick examination on me, so I had to lie up on a bed on my side and pull my pants down.

He put on gloves and rubbed gel over his fingers, and said I was about to feel some pressure in my bum. *Oh lord, here we go!'*

Up the finger went; it only lasted about 10 seconds but it was enough for him to find out that my prostate was a bit swollen. I still paid no real heed, it was just a gland as far as I was concerned and there was no panic on me at all.

But it meant a biopsy the following month, and again I just went about my business at work and in full swing playing football with Aughnasheelin again. I was taking life in my stride without a care in the world.

My partner Linda came with me when it was time for the biopsy, and they took 16 samples of my prostate during the procedure. It's not a nice feeling, but it is what it is. After about an hour and a half of waiting around for me to pass urine, I was told I could go home and I'd get a call when the results came back.

The whole thing is a long process, and we were told the results wouldn't come back until almost three months later as they had to be examined at a specialist laboratory.

The cell samples are sent to a lab and the simplest way to describe the process is that they have to ripen, to see what's actually happening with the prostate gland. But life still continued as normal, with no worries. The results lingered in the back of my mind, but cancer or anything like that wasn't in my head.

I had been through that battle already and won, but little did I know I would soon face it all over again.

« CHAPTER 14 »

THE MONTHS PASSED, with everything always in the back of my mind. Finally, in February 2016 the results were in.

A letter arrived informing me of an appointment to see Dr Garrett Durkan – a consultant urologist and surgeon in University College Hospital Galway again. He was the head man when it came to all this stuff.

Myself and Linda headed off in the car, as I stuck to my rule of never going for test results again by myself. There were a lot of people ahead of us in the waiting room when we arrived, which was far from ideal and we had a lot of time to kill.

But I knew from past experience that when you were called in to talk about results, they'd found something troublesome.

My heart was pounding when we were finally called in to see the doctor, and I could feel the sweat starting to come through my palms. There is nothing you can do when you are waiting for weeks or months for test results because you could drive yourself crazy otherwise, but this was crunch time.

I was even more nervous about this than I was running out at Croke Park 22 years beforehand to play the Dubs in the All-Ireland semi-final.

DR DURKAN WAS a gentleman and couldn't have put us more at ease, but the biopsy results were there in black and white and the news was bad.

Out of the 16 samples taken from my prostate, eight of them returned as cancerous, so I officially had prostate cancer. Just like the first time, I went into a daze. All of those horrible thoughts rumbled through my head – here we go again with chemotherapy, operations, being sick, losing my hair, having to give up football, my new job... even contemplating death... once more.

Surviving cancer the first time was great, but could I do it again? I genuinely didn't know. Thankfully Linda was there to take it on board with me and hear what Dr Durkan was saying, because when you are in a state of shock like that the room starts spinning.

He reassured us that I was in a good place, because the cancer was identified early and I had options, which was always good and that put my mind at ease a bit.

The hand I was dealt meant I could go for radiotherapy, brachytherapy or robotic surgery in terms of treatment. I looked up each one of them, and brachytherapy meant radioactive seeds would be implanted into my prostate to kill off the cancerous cells.

Radiotherapy basically did the same thing, and I was told that it could take 15 or 20 sessions in the hospital. Robotic surgery meant removing the prostate altogether in one procedure.

The next few weeks and months would all be down to another appointment in Galway to see what else was going on in my prostate.

The nurse in charge, Geraldine, was a huge help when I turned up for that appointment. She talked to me as a person, and helped me feel human instead of a number on a chart, because all of these visits can be painfully terrifying.

She kept me calm, and was really recommending the bracket therapy for me. In the back of my mind, typically all I could think about was football and work. I was young and healthy, but they had to see what size my prostate was to determine the best course of action – which meant an ultrasound exam.

The nurse gave me directions where to go, and said she would meet me down there. I descended down the corridor and opened the door, and wasn't sure if I was in the right room or not.

Inside was a bed with two leg stirrups at the end of it, and I knew I wasn't here to give birth even though I may have had a bit of a belly! I was nervously giggling to myself, praying that I was in the wrong place and someone was just having a laugh.

But despite the odd paraphernalia, it was the right room alright. Geraldine told me to put on the gown, pull down my pants and lie up on the bed and wait for the doctor.

She started to talk to me about where I was from and what I did with my life, and I mentioned working in the hospital, playing football, living in Sligo and life with Linda and everything else.

When the doctor arrived, much to my horror my legs had to go up on the stirrups, and Geraldine was over by my shoulder. It was time to give birth, but something was about to go in, as opposed to come out.

Before I knew it, I could feel the pressure of what was the bar by the bedside going up my back passage to measure my prostate.

Geraldine kept talking in order to distract me from what was going on, and started chatting away to me about my football career, as if we were meeting for a cup of tea! But I told her it didn't matter what she said, because nothing could distract me from this cold bar with a condom on it going up my arse.

Geraldine was laughing to lighten the mood, but there was only so much you could sugar-coat what was going on. It lasted no more than two minutes but it felt like two hours. Finally, the job was done and the mini-invasion was over. We went back up to Dr Durkan's room and he soon arrived with good news.

My prostate was the right size to go ahead with brachytherapy if I wanted to, but I had to make another appointment with him again first. Another few weeks passed and as we went into March it was time to see him again, and this time I knew he wanted to talk to me about robotic surgery.

I booked the day off work and Linda set off for Galway with me again. We decided to go down the night before. Driving into Galway in the morning with traffic and roadworks, and everything else can be a hindrance. It can just be a very long day, between the journey up and down and the three or four hours you spend in the hospital, between waiting and being seen to and hitting the road again.

Going down early helped a bit, because we made a night of it before going in to see Dr Durkan.

He was already aware that I was leaning towards brachytherapy, as it meant a speedy solution and I could return to work and play football again with no huge lay-off, with a view to the cancer being gone again within a year.

He said it would do the job, but my prostate would still be there – and there was always a risk that the cancer could come back and cause more trouble.

My prostate was the right size for brachytherapy alright, but it was also a manageable size for robotic surgery to get it out of there completely, which meant any future hassle would be avoided. I would go under the knife, be kept in for three or four days and the prostate would be out and gone along with all the cancer too.

He told me to go home and ponder it, and return the following week with a decision. There was no pressure on me, and it was entirely up to myself. It was just a case of choosing one or the other and despite the simplicity of it, there was still a very important decision to be made.

Over the course of that weekend, I could hardly eat or sleep as this choice dominated my thoughts. It was either going to save my life or not, and making the right call was crucial.

Do I get rid of the prostate or keep it there and risk the cancer coming back again?

Working in the hospital helped, because I had the ear of a few doctors in there and I asked them what they thought. I also confided in my brother to ask his doctor – I wanted as many informed opinions as possible before deciding what to do.

But just like asking the audience a handy question in *Who wants to be a Millionaire?* Ninety-nine percent of them said to get rid of the prostate and stick it in the bin for good.

MY MIND WAS made up then. It meant time off work and a break from football to have the surgery and recover, and also changes to my waterworks, but the prostate would be gone forever and all the worries that went with it.

I told Dr Durkan to fire ahead and take it out using robotic surgery. The next step was to wait for the appointment to go under the knife once more.

Linda said it was a great way to lose weight, as I was gradually having all these body parts taken out of me… and my prostate was next up after losing one of my testicles. It meant a half a pound off the scales at least! I always laugh at my own expense, but that's just me! But deep down, I knew I was making the right call. Everyone was telling me as much, and I could worry about the recovery and any of the side effects when the time came. Beside the bed was a bar about a yard long and a box of condoms, and I was tempted to stick a few of them into my pocket for a rainy day!

I was to have the procedure on May 6, and it would last a couple of hours along with three or four days in hospital to heal up before heading home. But overall, the recovery wouldn't last too long.

I kept working right up until the operation, and my employers at TTM were excellent to me throughout the whole process. I would need two or three months off in total, and they were fully supportive of me and are an absolute pleasure to deal with when any health issues arise.

Had I not needed a fit to work letter to start working with them in the first place, the prostate cancer would not have been spotted so early, even though I was getting my bloods taken every six months religiously anyway.

I was told to check into University College Hospital in Galway, and recover there before being sent home.

A few weeks passed and the letter arrived, but it said the surgery was to take place at the Galway Clinic – the fancy private hospital on the outskirts of the city near the M6 motorway to Dublin.

I packed my bag and hit the road with Linda again. When we arrived at the clinic, we parked up and the receptionist confirmed I was booked in there for my procedure. Curious as to my new grand surroundings, I asked them if I was staying there for the recovery and was told I was, which I was delighted with!

Even at that, I was still expecting to be sharing a public ward with four or five other patients – and I would have been happy enough with that. I arrived at my ward, and the station nurse guided me down to my room, which was a huge private room the size of a living room!

I was waiting for someone to come and tell me there'd been a mistake, and I couldn't understand why I was getting all this lavish treatment and comfort for my surgery.

But this is where my own job came in handy.

A big infection had spread in Sligo University Hospital a few weeks before my surgery, and to ensure I didn't carry it elsewhere I was shipped off to my new private digs at the Galway Clinic to minimise my contact with staff and other patients.

The seriousness of what was ahead of me never went away mind you, but I made the best of my little luxury break at the same time. There was a TV over the bed, and at the bottom of the bed were three or four towels with a bag of soaps and shampoos. Only around five minutes had passed when a chef from the kitchen came in and handed me a dinner menu with the best of grub on it. I was over the moon! Sleeping can be a great escape, but it dawned on me again what lay ahead as soon as I woke up and I remembered I was far from my own bed.

The thought of chemo again or even radiotherapy terrified me, and in these situations, there is a constant worry about what the future might hold – from small silly things to the worst case scenario.

The amount of information you are given through the whole thing is so helpful, but the bottom line is to prepare yourself for the worst, but just hope for the best. Dr Durkan arrived to tell me again what lay ahead and it was time to put on the silly gown, hat and knickers again, and off to the theatre I went. There was a lot of hooking up to be done before I went under the knife, and they connected me to a heart monitor… and a needle had to go into my wrist to keep an eye on my blood pressure during the procedure.

From there, it was lights out as they placed the anaesthetic mask over my mouth… and I failed to complete my countdown again. I felt okay once I came around again, and I had a new companion even though my prostate was gone.

I was now wearing a catheter, which is a device that takes urine from your bladder and drains it into a bag outside the body. I had to wear two of them – one for during the day and one for night time. Dr Durkan had explained all of this to me before the operation. But overall, I felt good bar a few aches and pains around my chest, joints and shoulders. The nurse gave me antibiotics and painkillers, and she said the soreness was a result of the gas that was pumped into my body to basically open me up so they could access my prostate.

They use a machine to take the prostate out, but the gas filters through your whole body and the impact of that results in around 12 hours of pain post-surgery.

The following day, Dr Durkan came in and told me it went very well even though the prostate had been a little larger than expected, but they got it all out of there safely. Mission accomplished. It was time to recover for the next few days, but I sure was enjoying being in that lovely private room and being fed the best of grub morning, noon and night. It was like staying in a hotel and getting constant room service, and I lapped it up!

AFTER DAY THREE, Dr Durkan returned to see how I was feeling. In the back of my mind, I wanted to squeeze one more night out of the place so I told him I was still a bit sore and my stay was extended.

They gave me loads of documentation and information on what was going to happen over the next few weeks and months, and I had to wear the catheter for a week to allow my insides to heal and my waterworks to start repairing themselves.

The day bag is your urine bag strapped around your kneecap, and you can go about your business and nobody is any the wiser as it gradually fills up. The night bag is designed to hang over the edge of your bed so you can sleep as normal.

I was walking around Sligo town a few days after I was discharged from the hospital just to pass the time and dander around the shops, and I could feel something pulling at me in my pants.

My day bag had come loose from around my knee, and was dangling around my ankle – full to the brim with urine!

I had to leg it somewhere to empty the bag, and I frantically made my way through the streets of Sligo before I found a laneway for refuge. People were looking at me as if I had two heads, but I ignored them in my state of emergency.

I eventually jumped in behind a car, and put my leg out like a dog would do going to the toilet to open the bag and empty it out onto the street.

It was the only way I could relieve the pressure and put the bag back towards my knee and strap it back on. I think nobody saw me, or at least I hope so!

When you're wearing the bag, you nearly forget you have it on as it sits silently doing a job for you, even though it has the potential to go horribly wrong like it did that day in Sligo town, but it could have always been worse.

Another nine days passed before I had the catheter removed, and the nurse pulled it out at a snail's pace, which was far from pleasant. One of the big side effects of having your prostate being removed is urinary incontinence, and not being able to control your bladder for weeks and months on end. You are given a booklet for exercises to do to get the system working again as normal, so you can regain some form of control.

You get another leaflet explaining the side-effects, and one telling how to deal with the emotional side of things after the operation, because you are wearing a pad for the initial period of time to control your urine and it can be very stressful.

The nurse had given me loads of extra pads to wear, and a box of Viagra. The last thing I was thinking about at the time was getting down to business! But I had to take them to help the muscles down there get back to normal, and it takes a while for them to get working again. The Viagra tablets weren't for me to have a good time that night at all!

The exercises consisted of floor movements and pelvic workouts to aid your muscles around your bladder and groins, which also help to control your waterworks which I never knew at all, and most people don't.

It took a long time for me to get my bladder back working fully again so that I didn't need a pad. It's just one of the common side effects that men have after having their prostate removed and it's a lot to take on board over an extended period of time. Sometimes it's embarrassing, especially having to wear a pad on your groin area to keep yourself dry like an adult nappy.

I've had friends ring me who have been through the same thing asking me how long it lasts post-surgery, and I just have to be honest and tell them it can last for weeks or even months, and it just depends on how quickly it all heals.

Obviously, everyone is different, and some patients have to contend with it for much longer than others. Thankfully, at this stage in my recovery there was no decision to be made around radiotherapy, or the dreaded chemotherapy that left me wanting to die during my first cancer ordeal.

Needless to say, it would have been horrendous to go through that again but the chances of that were slim. The number one aim was to just get rid of the prostate, then wait a month to take a blood test to see how the numbers were shaping up.

All going to plan, the PSA figures would be back to normal. But it's always in the back of your mind how this will pan out, and even Dr Durkan didn't know what lay in store until we got the numbers in black and white.

There's always the question around if the cancer had spread before the prostate was removed, and it's a horrifying thought. You just hope that everything is caught early, and that it was all taken away during the surgery. Every angle was covered for getting back to full strength but I had to do what I was told in terms of relaxing, recovering, doing the exercises and being aware of what I'd just been through.

Had I gone back to work or a football field, I would have done more damage and it would have been reckless and under no circumstances could I bite off more than I could chew.

Six weeks or so passed and I spent a lot of time chilling out and recovering before I went back to Dr Durkan again to have my bloods taken to see the lie of the land. I let my body steadily heal by itself through the summer, and as usual my mother was firing all these remedies at me to speed up the process, and my brother was constantly urging me to keep drinking mint tea to heal my system.

I gave it a go, but the smell of it alone put me off, and I said after one sip I was sticking to my normal tea with a drop of milk and a few biscuits and a bit of cake, if there was any going!

I JUST WANTED to let my body heal in my own way, and trust the process and the science behind everything I had been told by the experts.

But my grandmother had great healing power, and for some reason after every operation I've had I seem to recover more quickly than most people, so her magic must have passed on to me in some shape or form.

I let my body repair itself naturally, and I went fishing for perch and pike around Drumshanbo, went for walks, went to club matches and I felt good because all of those things really helped me to switch off and put this latest ordeal in the back of my mind.

I had returned to work the week before going back to Galway to see Mr Durkan. My area manager Sandra McMahon was delighted to have me back in action, but I was conscious of not overdoing it given the job entails a lot of lifting and moving and physical activity.

My colleagues welcomed me back with open arms, and quizzed me constantly about my procedure and my recovery with fascination.

They all admired my resolve, and a lot of them called me a warrior. I love my job, and I find it very rewarding, so getting back to action was a dream. I was no longer a patient when I was at work, and I was helping others instead.

When I went back to Dr Durkan, my blood results were good, thank God. My prostate PSA levels were 00.1, which was a huge relief! He showed me a diagram of where my cancer was, and he determined that it occurred inside the walls of the now removed prostate. That meant it had not spread, and catching it so early, along with the levels that came back from the blood test meant no radiotherapy or chemotherapy either!

That was amazing news, because the thought of being back in bed for days on end with no hair, energy or desire to live was beyond frightening.

All I could visualise was my head in the toilet getting sick, puking into a bucket, always being down and just constantly feeling horrible. I don't know if I would have been able to face that again, and thankfully it's a question I didn't have to answer.

HAVING THE PROSTATE removed was absolutely the right call because we got it early, and now normality was in sight again and the light was at the end of the tunnel.

I had to get my bloods taken every three months in Galway with Dr Durkan for the first two years after that, and every time a sample was taken the prostate level stayed at 00.1, much to my delight.

I asked him if I could get the tests done in Sligo to save me the journey going forward, and if anything was suspicious, I'd come straight back to Galway to see him, and thankfully he agreed. It just made life a bit easier and saved the hassle of travelling up and down and organising time off with work.

To this day, I make sure and get my bloods taken every six months regardless if I have a leg hanging off me or I'm as sick as a dog.

I was told at the very beginning that it might be a pain in the arse doing it twice a year, but if you leave the system and a couple of years pass and there's something wrong with you, you have to start from scratch and go through the whole process again to get seen.

I'm in the system now. They have all my records and I go for my bloods every six months, and God forbid, if they find something wrong, they can nail it immediately. It's just about staying on top of things.

Doctors and nurses and all of the healthcare staff in this country don't get half the credit they deserve for the amazing work they do.

Getting checked out straightaway had saved my life, and I had beaten cancer for a second time.

My football career in 2016 was a write-off with the procedure, and I thought I had officially retired then.

After facing another terrifying ordeal and coming out the right side of it, there was no chance I was giving up football now. Beating cancer once was incredible, and I was beyond elated to do it again. I was back playing before I knew it, and people recognised it was such an incredible story.

When you have beaten cancer twice, it's even more astounding and quite overwhelming. You get this sense that nothing can put you down any more, and you'll overcome whatever comes at you.

You get all this attention and people are looking at you as this guy on the field who has lived to tell the tale, and people half my age have given up on football because they can't commit or they don't enjoy it. But I just love it, and representing your home club again after beating cancer twice is just amazing.

I always worry that it might come back, of course I do. I'm always conscious of it when I'm getting my bloods taken, but I always feel confident. There's always a little voice at the back of my mind that is saying they might find something again. After having it twice, I am prone to it coming back. *Is that a worry?* Yes, big-time. But if it does, I'll attack it with the same approach, hit it head on and fight it.

And don't get me wrong, I am well aware that countless people don't have the same luck that I had.

I just enjoy life now. I love working in the hospital, helping the patients and every day I get out of bed and get back into it that night is a good day for me. If it's a case that I get cancer again, and I only have six months to live, those six months will be lived to the last and I'll have a bucket list the length of my arm – including climbing Mount Everest.

But beating cancer the second time was my Everest in so many ways. I don't know what is going to happen next week, next month or next year.

I see people in my job who are my age now or younger than me having strokes, heart attacks and being diagnosed with a terminal illness, and they are gone to their eternal reward in less than six months.

That goes to show just how lucky I was that I caught cancer early. If anyone finds something it must be nailed on the head straight away. If you don't, it could come back and bite you.

That's why if I have a thousand more minutes on the field, I will enjoy every second of it. You never know when that last minute will come.

The final whistle does blow for us all eventually, and there is no escaping that.

PART **SIX**

The Impossible Dream

*Age has never mattered to me...
I've always wanted to play, make
those saves, kick the ball as far
as I can... and let out a few yells
at my defenders.*

« CHAPTER 15 »

DESPITE ALL THAT was going on with the prostate removal, I made it my business to be around the club a lot in 2016.

I watched from the wings as the lads started brilliantly and topped their group in the championship with three wins against Fenagh, Eslin and Glenfarne-Kiltyclogher.

We went through to the knockout stages, but Ballinaglera ended our interest in the quarter-finals and that was that. I was just happy to be there, knocking around the place, as it gave me a purpose but inside it was silently killing me not being able to tog out and take part in training or play the matches.

But if I did risk it, there was a chance I would push myself too hard and doing that could have really meant the end in terms of my playing career that I was so dearly holding on to.

As hard as it was, I had to know my limits and stay in my lane, and in hindsight it was certainly the way to go.

I eventually went back to playing local soccer in Sligo with Merville United; again to pass the winter that year, and we won a league title which was great. I also started playing over-40s football and lined out for the Leitrim Masters team. It's a competition for men who want to keep playing football but are maybe past their sell by date at club level and are battling with their bellies a bit!

When you get to a certain age, younger and fitter players are constantly coming behind you as the next generation filters through and a new panel takes shape. I had dipped my toes into Masters football in 2009. I remember lining out against Mayo and Dublin not long after winning the Longford title with Clonguish.

We beat the Dubs, and I remember it well because a row broke out. Dublin being Dublin had a few all-time greats on the field, and at one stage one of them, who had filled that iconic blue jersey, trampled across the field to get stuck in once the skirmish broke out.

IN 2016 I went back to Masters football and by then there was an amalgamated team between Leitrim and Longford just to make up the numbers. It was pressure-free football and you were playing with and against players who were all at the same level. Some of those men are still freakishly fit, and the likes of Conor Gormley and Stephen O'Neill helped Tyrone win the 2021 All-Ireland for example.

Others have the beer bellies coming on strong, but it's always a great laugh and a great way to catch up with some old faces.

The competitions are run off between the All-Ireland Championship, the Shield and the Plate depending on where teams finish in group stages, so there's always something to play for.

For some reason, I was the only man from the Leitrim 1994 team on the amalgamated panel with Longford.

It's a great competition which is growing all the time, but sadly it is still waiting for official recognition from the GAA itself. We won the All-Ireland Shield, and it was great craic.

But as 2017 began, I wasn't up for playing anything at all. Between my age and everything I had been through, my body was starting to wave flags all over the place. Playing soccer in the winter was grand, but gaelic football was always that bit more serious – and David Casey from Boyle had taken over the team at Aughnasheelin.

Training had begun and I opted against it initially, but it wasn't long before I started missing it, along with the banter with the lads. I went on the 40 minute spin in the car and landed down one evening and that's where my unknown path to dreamland began.

Richie Fitzpatrick took the initiative and asked me to help out our goalkeepers Sean Mahon and Dean Flanagan, and several twists of fate would lead to what followed for the rest of the season.

Sean was roughly the same age as me, but Dean was first-choice so it was never even near my mind that I could return and fight for a jersey. But once I put on my boots and gloves and got out on the field, the bug was back – *does it ever really go away?*

Let's not beat about the bush here – I was struggling big-time to keep up with things at training, so helping the two lads out was definitely the right place for me on my initial return until I dusted off few cobwebs from my latest health ordeal.

The management were delighted I was there to help out and lend my expertise, but they had a plan in the back of their heads to really coax me back into playing again.

I slowly but surely got fitter, and started really enjoying things again. I eventually saw myself as the third-choice keeper, but bar a disaster I never thought for one second I would actually be required to play.

When the league began, I togged out, but was still largely there to help the goalkeepers and keep them on their toes. That's when it all kicked off as Dean hurt his hip in a league match, and Sean fell victim to a hamstring pull in the second-half after coming on to replace him.

I issued my colourful response when I was told to warm-up but I soon had no choice in the matter.

SUDDENLY, I HAD gone from goalkeeping coach and third-choice in case of an emergency to actually being back between the posts in a competitive match.

It was clear Dean and Sean would not be fit to play in our next league match the following week, so this 'last resort' closing in on 47 years of age was going to play again… me.

I even struggled in the warm-up as it was a fairly hot day. Football was a fast game now, and I was slow!

I just wasn't fit enough at that point to keep this going, but I got through it and we won the game against Fenagh. If I wanted to be No 1 and stay there, extra training would be needed but I found it really hard to motivate myself to get properly fit again given my age, and what I had been through in terms of my health and everything else.

I had one testicle, no prostate and it remained to be seen if I would be able for this at all. But our selector Richie Fitzpatrick still saw something in me, and was full of admiration for the effort I was putting in. He urged me to keep at it, and kept telling me that the cream would always rise to the top.

He stressed that I would be No 1 before the year was out regardless of how fit Dean and Sean were, if we were still there at the business end of the championship and I got myself to where I needed to be.

That's all well and good for a young lad, but not a fella pushing 50 really struggling to train and get to any sort of fitness level to compete in the modern game.

Richie wasn't the only one admiring my efforts in the midst of all these young lads, some of which were nearly 30 years younger than me. I had played with the fathers of some of my teammates!

The thought of the challenge and the encouraging words from those around me drove me on, and a new motivation filtered through me to make a real stab at this.

The media attention in the papers and on the radio came and went, and I did a few interviews as people started taking notice of my unintentional journey back into club football when all the signs were that it was over for me.

Coming up to the championship, Dean had returned to fitness and David cranked things up a notch at training – it wasn't too far off inter-county standard if I'm honest.

Everyone had to be there and commitment was paramount.

We trained in Bunbrosna during the week, which is between Mullingar and Edgeworthstown in Longford, to make life easier for the lads on the panel based in Dublin. David's standards were extremely high, and that was the making of us. The sessions would go on for around an hour and 45 minutes, and afterwards there would usually be food for us and ice baths to help with recovery.

Back in the day we were jumping into rivers to recover, but a lot of lads wouldn't go near the water! But David demanded we get into these ice baths to make sure there were no more niggles and that nothing would hamper his big plans for the championship.

I KEPT DOING my own thing and working hard, but just presumed I would not be the main goalkeeper in our bid for glory after losing in the quarter-finals the year before. Eventually, I was in good enough shape in time for the first round at the end of July, when we were in a six-team group with Fenagh, Ballinaglera, Drumkeeran, Eslin and Aughavas.

The top four qualified for the quarter-finals, and the bottom two went into relegation play-offs. If you topped your group, you played whoever finished fourth in the other group in the last eight, and so on.

David put a huge emphasis on topping the group undefeated, and we hammered Eslin and Drumkeeran in our first matches to put us in the driving seat straightaway. I was on the bench for those games as second-choice to Dean – unfortunately for him Sean's year was over at this stage.

From the line, I kept a really close eye on how our backline and Dean were playing, and I could see little errors here and there that were occurring during games. When the pressure was on, Dean was prone to panicking a little bit. He was making good saves and his kick-outs weren't too bad, but he would get the jitters the odd time under a high ball or if our opponents were enjoying a decent spell in the match. With the experience of playing in goals at a high level I noticed these small things, but dared not tell the manager.

We drew with Ballinaglera, before a dogged win over Aughavas, and our last group game was against Fenagh in Ballinamore. If we won, we would top the group and get an easier draw for the quarter-finals.

But we were losing coming down the stretch.

With around 15 minutes to go, the management must have lost a bit of confidence in Dean and the call came for me to warm-up. I said to myself... *Oh my sweet Jesus.*

I could feel my heart beating through the No 16 jersey, because this was the championship and there was a nice little crowd there watching on too. Never in a million years did I think I would play that day, and I only had a couple of minutes to warm-up before being thrown into it with the game in the melting pot.

I jumped and leapt along the sideline like a child, but damaged my ankle in the process! I said nothing because it wasn't too bad, but it did create a little bit of panic in me because I thought it would hamper my kick-outs. But I eventually shook it off and I was alright.

I trudged on, handed my slip to the referee and he laughed and said 'You're not still at it McHugh!' I just told him to go easy on me. A nice little cheer rippled across the supporters as I made my way to my old home in the small square.

My heart was in my mouth and I was shaking like a leaf, but I composed myself, gathered my thoughts and told myself to just do the simple things right until the end of the game and the rest would look after itself.

I had so much experience, but it counts for nothing when the nerves take hold of you like that and you've been away from playing for a long time.

A FEW KICK-OUTS came and went with no real disaster to report, and we got a goal to win the game, 3-9 to 2-9.

Most importantly, we had topped the group undefeated, just as David wished, to give us a real shot in the arm coming into the knockout stages.

From that moment on, I really pushed myself because I knew there could be no turning back now. We had a serious chance of doing something special. I was in bonus territory and this was my chance to stay No 1 for it all and finally get my hands on a championship medal with my home club.

The pressure was on to work a bit harder and really sharpen myself up, and I really had to view this as my last chance of playing football at a decent level and winning something notable while I was at it.

A club championship medal with Aughnasheelin was the glaring omission from my mantelpiece and achieving it was starting to come into view.

We only had eight days to get ready for our quarter-final showdown against Mohill, and David told us we would train in Lough Key Forest park that week – where I had put in so many of those hard yards with John O'Mahony and Leitrim 23 years beforehand.

We gathered in the car park, and I was getting flashbacks of Johno barking at us, before we were brought to a zipline area going through the trees. But we weren't there for the craic, and we walked on past it on to a path I knew well, because Johno had run the s***e out of us there back in the day.

We did a warm-up before David split us into two groups to go around the mile-and-a-half long track in different directions, before meeting back at the starting point. I felt like telling him to feck off, but once the whistle went the lads were gone – and after 10 seconds, I was behind them by myself, left for dust and Paddy last.

I came around a bend and the lads were all gone because they were flying it, but I eventually finished the run and the lads were there to push me on the final stretch.

David took a minute to speak, and commended what I was doing for the team and the club despite what I had been through and my obvious struggles. I had been to hell and back, so he insisted there were to be no excuses from anyone else on the panel.

That pushed me even further too, and we went around that track twice more before 15 short up-hill runs to close it out in the middle of that old forest. We were exhausted, but we all finished that session on a serious high – and my fitness and stamina were constantly improving.

David was thinking big, and wanted to make sure that if we got to a final, we'd be ready for it. We edged Mohill by a point in Ballinamore, and were given plenty to think about in a 0-13 to 1-9 win, because it was a real dogfight.

Losing that game would have been a huge upset, and it looked like a replay was on the cards before Gavin McWeeney dramatically won it for us four minutes into injury time. Ryan Murphy scored a goal for Mohill in the first minute much to my disgust, but Fintan Fitzpatrick was outstanding for us before Gavin came off the bench to be the hero and see us through.

We were 0-10 to 1-0 up at half-time and we were cruising, but Mohill won the second half 0-9 to 0-3! It was a real warning sign and we were extremely lucky not to be knocked out that evening.

We had another fortnight before the semi-final against Carrigallen, who had finished second in the other group. We were a wounded dog after what happened in the last eight, and we hit them for 1-5 to put ourselves in the driving seat early doors – Fergal Earley got our goal.

We had eight different scorers and I kept a clean sheet in a 1-16 to 0-10 victory in Ballinamore again.

We slacked off a bit in the second-half once more which was a worry, but we were into the final and that was all that mattered. From here, the hype in the village went into overdrive before the big day against Leitrim Gaels in another two weeks.

Preparing for a county final with your own home club was just on a different level to anything else, and incredibly special.

I had won those medals with Clonguish, but home is always home; it's where you grew up and you are soldiering with your friends and neighbours, or in my case at this stage a lot of their sons.

I loved the buzz about the place, especially going into championship week when the village was decked in green and white flags and banners all over the place.

I just never thought I would see the day, especially at my age and the lift it had already given the parish was just huge. Leitrim Gaels had won the other semi-final against Drumkeeran, and were slight favourites heading into the game against us in Carrick.

We trained the weekend before the match, and Willie Donnellan from the *Leitrim Observer* came to one of our sessions to take some photographs.

He took a lovely snap of myself, Sean and Dean together. The sessions at that stage were mainly just to sharpen up on a few things, talk about our game plan and get into the zone for the opposition.

My job was to get my kick-outs right and counteract the height of some of the Leitrim Gaels players. They had a few lads who were over six feet tall, and I had to make sure they didn't utilise that from my restarts.

I made sure I got plenty of work done with my backs and midfielders, especially under a high ball because the Gaels could really punish us there with their height. David was determined to leave no stone unturned to win this game, and so were we. Becoming champions was only a game away, and all of our hard work would count for nothing if we fell at the last hurdle.

County hit-man Aidan Flynn was the Leitrim Gaels star forward and would take watching, and that would prove to be the case on the day.

THE MORNING OF the game finally arrived, and by that point we all had schedules for the day and what to eat from the moment we woke up. I had a nice breakfast of porridge, tea and a few sly biscuits, and drank plenty of water before heading towards Carrick.

My gear was all ready and Linda was coming to the match as well – she was very excited for me that morning as well before I hit the road.

And sure enough, I think I stopped twice between home and Carrick to double check that everything was in my gear bag!

I was still that freak, double or even triple checking things, and having spare gear. *Do I have my boots? Spare boots? Gloves? Shorts?* I would check again and again and again just to make sure nothing was missing.

I got there well over an hour before the game and, once I arrived, I relaxed a bit because my gear checks and worries over being late were out of my system. A few heads from home were already there to support us. I had a chat with a few of them and it was all nice and chilled out at that stage.

There was no point in getting uptight and stressed out about things now. I had been through all of this before. The work was done across the panel. I was in good shape myself and all we had to do was work hard for 60 minutes and get the result we wanted.

We got into the dressing-room and there were drinks, sweets and fruit waiting for us to keep us fuelled up for the afternoon. I was cracking jokes that they were laid out for a party, and silently hoped I wasn't jinxing us.

We warmed-up out on the field behind the main stand, and Sean and Dean helped me loosen up as we went through some drills and practiced some more kick-outs. I was very relaxed and in the zone, and we went back into the dressing-room for one last pep talk before throw-in.

David and his selectors started talking, and before long we got a knock on the door from the fourth official to come out on the field, but the lads kept on yapping and barking out instructions.

I was getting a bit worked up at this point, because I wanted enough time to get a few more practice kick-outs away on the main pitch before it was time for action.

We were a couple of minutes late leaving the dressing-room, and that's when we had to wait in the tunnel, because Leitrim Gaels were on time and were going out before us instead.

The nerves were really building now. When you are ready to run out, it's best to go there and then, but when you are held up like that, even a minute can seem like an eternity.

Energy levels can he sapped in an instant, and that's when I turned around and roared…

'THIS IS IT LADS!

'WE ARE ABOUT TO RUN ON TO THAT FIELD AND BE GREETED BY 1,500 PEOPLE FROM OUR OWN PARISH.

'SUCK IT UP

'DON'T LET THE NERVES GET TO YOU!

'THIS IS WHAT WE CAME HERE FOR!'

This was for us… our team, our families and our village.

It was up to us to go and win and when we eventually did get out there, we were greeted by an unmerciful cheer.

We posed for a team photo and I can still remember Willie Donnellan telling me to smile! 'F**k you Willie!' was my giddy reply, and we went through the final motions before throw-in and we were off.

MYSELF AND MY defenders fully expected the Gaels to pump in high balls to try and outdo us in the air, and we had a shaky enough start.

We gave away a lot of ball, but still got a few points on the board as Conor Cullen started to come into his own at midfield, and largely nullified where the Gaels were expected to hurt us the most.

Our opponents were sluggish in front of goal, and would finish the game with 10 wides. I barely touched the ball in the first-half apart from kick-outs, which any goalkeeper should be delighted with.

I was often forced to go long to Conor, and it was largely paying off as he kept winning his own ball and running at them to set up our own attacks. He was brilliant, and would score three points himself too.

We led 0-7 to 0-4 at half-time, but it could have been more because their 'keeper Brendan Flynn saved a Barry McWeeney penalty, and somehow stopped the rebound as well to keep his team in it. It was a huge moment.

We were far off our best, but we were motoring along nicely. I often spoke in the dressing-room at the break but didn't this time, so David said his few bits and off we went again with a three-point lead to kick on with for the next half an hour or so.

We improved, and Niall Mulvanerty and Fintan Fitzpatrick put us five points up. Conor kept excelling for us, and won three of my kick-outs in-a-row to really hurt them and stall their hopes of a revival.

Aidan Flynn was still giving us problems and would finish with five points, and I had to start varying my kicks as the game progressed because they eventually decided to double-mark Conor in the middle because of all the damage he was doing.

With around 10 minutes to go, as I glanced over at the scoreboard, I had a sudden surge of excitement lifting through my stomach at the thought of winning the game. I just couldn't help it.

Emotions took over and I could feel myself tearing up, but I had to regain my composure and convince myself to calm down because the game was still on and very much in the melting pot.

The Gaels started their inevitable late charge and reeled us in a bit, and there was only a point in it coming down the stretch. I remember standing over a kick-out late on and having nobody to aim at, and referee Gareth Foley gave a hop-ball because I took too long. I was raging.

'F**K!' I roared at myself. But who else but Conor came in for the throw-up and regained possession and won a free out. He had totally saved my bacon.

One of our selectors, Damian Flynn, came in off the line towards me and issued some harsh words, and I knew I had gotten away with what could have been a very costly mistake. For every kick-out after that, I just hoofed it down the field towards Conor to get the ball away in the hope that he would keep winning it.

We were still a point up, but this was where things got scrappy and the Gaels started losing the heads.

A flashpoint arrived in stoppage time when the Gaels were infuriated by a sideline ball awarded our way, and the ball was brought forward and onto the field by the ref, who awarded us a free in.

Our opponents were livid, and even more so when Barry McWeeney stuck it beautifully over the bar.

We won their resulting kickout, and the final whistle blew.

0-12 to 0-10.

I fell to my knees and cried like a baby once more. We had done it!

There's nothing like a win like that to stir up all sorts of emotions, and I cried even more that day than I did after the 1994 Connacht final win with Leitrim.

I HAD PUT my body through so much for this.

I had beaten cancer twice and somehow achieved a Leitrim championship medal with lads almost 30 years younger than me.

It was pure raw emotion, and it took almost two minutes there and then, on my knees in front of my goal, as our jubilant supporters raced on to the pitch and patted me on the back.

Eventually, I got up and ran around to my teammates, with tears still streaming down my face, as the whole parish descended on the field. It was simply glorious.

It was an incredible moment when we went up the steps and Barry lifted the cup, as we gazed down at our ecstatic supporters basking in the glory of it all.

I had been giving Castlerahan in Cavan a hand again that year with some goalkeeping coaching, and they had reached the county final as well on the same day. Donal Keogan was managing them, and I was working with their goalkeepers Ciaran Daly and Jamie Leahy.

Donal was an old friend and, as I mentioned earlier, he had been manager of the Cavan minor and seniors and I knew him from those days. Ciaran was younger and a bit raw, and it looked like Jamie was primed to be first-choice.

We won the league before the championship, but they lost the county final 0-13 to 0-8 against Cavan Gaels, though they didn't let that defeat stall their progress. They would go on to win their first ever title in 2018, and retained their crown a year later.

Thankfully, there was something to celebrate that night with Aughnasheelin, and boy did we do that.

The party was being planned as soon as we eventually got back to the dressing-room after a nice length of time sharing those moments with our supporters out on the field.

These were the people we grew up with! The people who came to support me when my father died! Who were there when I was playing for Leitrim in big championship games all over the country, from Carrick-On-Shannon to Croke Park.

There's no better feeling, and four or five people came up to me and said how proud my father would have been to see this, and that he was looking down on me that day, a very happy man. I have no doubt that he was.

For so long, I was the Aughnasheelin man on the county team.

People young and old looked up to me; they were proud of what I achieved in the county colours but this was even better, and the perfect way to repay all of that support.

It's a team game and the lads were brilliant, but I doubt there are many others in Ireland who achieved that at my age after coming through all of those battles on and off the pitch.

BONFIRES LIT OUR path into the village, and it was just so exciting and such a great feeling to be returning to our little parish as champions, back where it all began with the cup on board.

There were bonfires outside my old school where those epic games were played out in the yard, and another outside the church.

We had a meal in Freddie's in Ballinamore and I went home after that to freshen up a bit and get changed.

I was tired and needed to recharge before going back to join the party, and within two hours of my return everyone was absolutely hammered drunk as the celebrations went into overdrive.

The cup was being passed around and it was full to the brim with alcohol, and despite calls from all the lads for me to take a sip, I wanted to stick with my Club Orange.

But I eventually gave in to taste this deadly cocktail of God knows what, and a huge cheer went up around the bar as my face soured in disgust at drinking this mix of utter poison.

WORK WITH TTM had been great with me all year too. I was able to do the shifts that suited me and win, lose or draw I had the Monday after that game off work with no issues at all.

A message went out on the WhatsApp group that we were to bring the cup to the school on the Monday, and then out to a retirement home in Ballinamore.

When we turned up at the school that morning, I wasn't sure whether to laugh or cry, because the bulk of the boys were still well drunk from the night before and some of them hadn't been to bed at all!

I got a great feeling being back in the school where I fell in love with the ball, and over 40 years later I returned with the cup.

That weekend it was back down to earth and back to training though. We were paired against Sligo champions St John's in the Connacht Intermediate Club championship quarter-final just two weeks after our victory.

But I really didn't want to play and urged David to start with Dean. A few key players were struggling with injuries and fatigue after investing so much into winning the Leitrim championship. At this stage, a provincial campaign was just bonus territory.

The preparation wasn't the same as it was for the county final, and I knew how good St John's were from living in Sligo and I knew we'd be up against it.

It was a really s****y day of rain and really strong wind, and the game was pulled from Markievicz Park in Sligo town over issues with the pitch. The match was a disaster; we were destroyed 3-12 to 0-3 at the Connacht Centre of Excellence in Bekan, just outside Ballyhaunis in Co Mayo.

Barry was our only scorer with three frees, so we failed to score from open play and the game was over in a flash as we just went through the motions until the final whistle. League of Ireland legend Alan Keane was playing for them, and the former Sligo Rovers and Dundalk defender caused havoc and scored 1-5. They had former Sligo stalwart Charlie Harrison at the back as well; they were just far too good for us.

We had put everything into winning the Leitrim championship and we didn't have a prayer as I looked on at the onslaught from the bench.

David wanted to throw me on for the last 10 minutes or so as one last reward for my work all year, but I refused. It was time to move on and let Dean continue as first-choice going forward.

I had nothing left to give. The game was a non-event for the most part because of the gulf in class. As I sat there, I thought back on the year and my life in football. I had a fair idea I wouldn't be able to achieve any more.

Maybe it was time to take a step back and count my medals. I left that pitch fairly convinced that was my last hurrah.

LEITRIM LEGEND COLIN Regan, who works for the GAA, writes a column with the *Leitrim Observer* and his piece that week contained a great photo of me shaking hands with former Leitrim chairman Gerry McGovern after the game.

Gerry then progressed to become president of the Connacht Council, and Colin waxed lyrical in his column about my career and was full of praise for my efforts down through the years.

Gerry is a lovely man who tells it as it is, and it's been great to see him rise through the ranks as an administrator in the GAA. In the back of my mind during that handshake, I thought that was it for me in terms of playing… I was done and dusted.

But the year still wasn't over. I had been nominated in a special achievement category for the Leitrim Sports Star Awards which were taking place at the end of November.

I thought it was just great to be considered, and I got an invitation for Linda and myself to attend the ceremony at the fabulous Lough Rynn Castle in Mohill. A host of individuals, teams and school teams from a wide range of sports from across the county were honoured on the night.

Local broadcaster John Lynch was MC and Connacht and Irish rugby legend Eric Elwood was Guest of Honour, and Irish international sprinter Eanna Madden won the overall award on the night.

When it came to the Special Achievement category and the names were listed out, I was chosen as a joint-winner along with Michael Cornyn.

Michael was originally from Ballinaglera and won gold, silver and bronze at the world masters indoor athletics championships in South Korea that year at the age of 56 – which was an astounding achievement and nothing short of incredible.

Michael went up first and I followed, and for the first time ever I was actually stuck for words when Johno was talking to us on stage.

It was another moment of personal pride, and not long after that our Leitrim championship medal presentation with Aughnasheelin took place at the Landmark Hotel in Carrick-on-Shannon.

I wasn't called up to collect my medal until last. After a nice meal the lads started to get into party mode again and a few more awards were handed out to people across the club who kept the whole thing going in the background. It was a nice moment to receive it from our club president Packie Mulvey, who has since passed on.

John Lynch was MC again, and the club made their own surprise presentation to me for my efforts that season. Once more, I was gobsmacked. For the second time in the space of a couple of weeks, I was speechless and incredibly emotional to go with it.

It just hit home again that I had achieved so much, and that this was probably going to be the last medal I would ever collect.

It was a nice moment to receive it from our club president Packie Mulvey, who has sadly since gone to his eternal reward with so many others who kept the club alive down through the years.

This was for all of them.

« CHAPTER 16 »

LIFE HAS BEEN great in the five years since all the chaos.

I'm still working three or four shifts a week. I'm involved with my beloved club and have branched into giving talks to various groups of people about my story.

I think it's important to spread cancer awareness – and especially testicular cancer. It's so common, yet it's still a fairly taboo subject for the bog-standard middle-aged male in particular in this country.

When it comes to talking about their testicles and their prostate, most men do not want to know and switch the subject to football or the weather to block it out and avoid it.

But I wanted to share my story to help others, and the first talk I gave was back at my old secondary school at St Felim's College in Ballinamore in October 2017.

It came about from a conversation I had one day on a break at work in the hospital in Sligo when people were quizzing me about my absence during my prostate cancer diagnosis. I told them I had been diagnosed with prostate cancer, and naturally mentioned my fight with testicular cancer before that, and they were gripped and astounded by what I was telling them.

Given they all work in healthcare, my colleagues urged me to share my story more widely, and that got me thinking about looking into speaking about it publicly and spreading awareness among men of all ages.

I wasn't sure where to start, but I rang St Felim's, now called Ballinamore

Community School, and got talking to the principal Padraig Leyden, a man from Fenagh and he said I could come in and chat to the transition year students about both of my battles.

Initially I thought I had bitten off more than I could chew, and that maybe it was a silly idea or it wouldn't happen at all. I'm not sure why, but cold feet took hold.

Padraig knew my story, and was even more aware of my endeavours on the football pitch and in fairness to him, he was all for it.

The night before I was due to go in, I was jotting down notes and thinking about how I would approach things and tell the story to this group of teenagers.

I was getting bogged down thinking about flip charts and all sorts of silly things and getting worked up and flustered. But Linda suggested I just go and tell it as it was, and exactly how it happened.

ALL I HAD to do was stand up and say what I went through, how it came about and how I recovered and take things from there.

Overthinking it all would get me nowhere, so I emptied my head and threw the notes I wrote into the bin, and that was the best preparation of all. I turned up at the school at around 10am and met a lady called Rachel was also there because she gives talks around the country on breast cancer awareness.

There were about 40 students present to hear what I had to say, and I knew a few of the teachers and staff – one of whom was an old neighbour from home, Peter Flynn.

I was naturally introduced as the former Leitrim goalkeeper and once I got up and started talking, I cracked a silly joke and all of the students laughed. The sound of that laughter eased all of my nerves, and away I went.

I spoke for nearly an hour, and the first thing I do now after every talk is get some feedback before I leave the room. I was delighted to get some great questions from those students in Ballinamore, and they all applauded when I finished up. That put a smile on my face and word got out in the community about my talk, and a few more schools got in touch in the coming weeks inviting me to come in and share my story with them too.

Getting that first talk out of the way cleared a path for me to keep at it and do more to spread awareness of my experience in the hope that it can help others.

Every year since then the same schools invite me back to tell it all over again to the next class of transition year students.

I even went into a few work-places and offices, like Sligo County Council, and I really enjoyed that as well. But overall, the talks have been fantastic and seem to have genuinely had a positive impact across the board.

Someone suggested that I speak to football teams as well, but I was apprehensive about that because I know what it's like inside that bubble. All you are thinking about is the next match, so someone speaking to a panel about testicular or prostate cancer might be a bit off the wall.

I just felt it might not be the right environment for a talk that could take up to an hour on a very serious subject.

But it turned out I was well off the mark on that one, because I got a huge response when I spoke to Drumkeeran GAA in Leitrim. Helping people is so rewarding, and having a few laughs with it helps with the stigma a bit. In every single case, most of the people in the room have been impacted by cancer in some regard, whether a family member, a friend or even themselves have had to deal with it in some shape or form.

It affects every single person you meet, and people can really relate to it when you humanise it… and actually humourise it a bit as well. When it comes to testicular cancer, I urge lads to check themselves out when they are in the shower and have a good feel – not a good time, but a good feel!

That usually gets a few laughs, but people seem to listen to it and take it on board as well, which is the most important thing. It's just to make sure everything is in order and there are no lumps or bumps.

A couple of times in the wake of my talks, gentlemen have ended up actually finding something on their testicles and getting themselves checked out. For every group I give a talk to, if I get through to and help even only a handful people I'll be happy.

It's basically the same talk every time, and I've never had anyone walk out yet. The bulk of those listening seem genuinely interested and intrigued by what they are hearing. And crucially, the bottom line is to keep an eye on things and if something is found, not to put it on the long finger. Get it checked out.

IN 2018 I visited Finner camp in Donegal, which is a military base for the Irish Defence Forces between Ballyshannon and Bundoran, not far from the Leitrim border. I turned up early and another gent was talking before me, and when I scoped out the room I could see some of the lads in the audience were quickly losing interest in what he was saying.

Thankfully, when I got up, the yawning stopped and nobody was looking at the clock, much to my relief. Whatever it is about my story, people seem to genuinely listen and take on board what I am saying.

I joked about trying not to get an erection as the nurses were feeling my testicles and things going up my bum to examine my prostate, but the serious nature of it all still carries the whole way through the chat.

I urge people to check themselves, and bring someone in with them when they are going to see a doctor or to an appointment. I use all of my experience each time I tell my tale.

I get a mixed bag of reactions from people, depending on the age of the audience. Older men over the age of 50 don't seem to want to hear stuff like that as much because it's probably a bit more taboo for them, but the students of today seem to be a bit more open-minded about it all.

Women are a lot more open to talking about this kind of thing when it comes to breast cancer or cervical checks and all of that, but adult men just prefer to chat about football, farming and the weather or anything but their health and well-being.

Mary and Bridget will chat away all day about their bits and pieces, but Paddy and Mickey do not want to hear it, if that makes sense, and the match at the weekend or the stretch in the evening will do them just fine as a conversation topic.

We are slowly getting there as men, and whenever older lads talk to me about their own ordeals they find it to be a huge weight off their shoulders, but more can always be done when it comes to talking about these things.

Over 200 students listened to me speak at Summerhill College in Sligo town, and I got a great laugh from the lads at Roscommon CBS too.I met them at the Abbey Hotel in Roscommon the last time I spoke to them just to make sure we could all remain socially distanced because of Covid-19.

When I asked the room how many people had known someone who had dealt with some form of cancer, every single person raised their hand. When the students asked questions at the end, one of them asked if I could still have sex even though I had one testicle!

The entire room erupted with laughter, teachers included and I was laughing so much it took me over two minutes to answer him. I gleefully told him the answer was yes, much to the delight of the room!

I am asked all sorts of questions, from had I thought of death... to could I replace the testicle I had removed!

I do have to remind people that I'm always in fear of my cancer returning, and that my blood tests every six months are vital, and thankfully have been all good so far. But you are always thinking in the back of your head that the day could come when something crops up, because it has happened to me twice already. But when I'm waiting for the results, I'm always positive, and that's vital too.

Actually telling my story could easily stop me in my own tracks when I hear myself telling it back or returning to some of those dark days, but it doesn't. It just makes me think of what I actually went through, especially when I was going through chemotherapy and felt that I wanted to die.

Those dark days will always live with me, and reliving that in my head can be a frightening experience.

THINKING OF PEOPLE I knew who never lived to tell the tale can be upsetting, and everyone you meet is in that boat whether it be losing family members or friends.

This subject is very real, it's out there and it can impact anyone at any time. I do the talks off my own bat in my spare time. I've been doing them for nearly five years already, and it's just a very fulfilling hobby.

In September 2018, one of our Castlerahan players Oisín Kiernan was diagnosed with testicular cancer, and he is a well-known Cavan footballer too.

The night we were told his news, he came up to me himself and enquired about what lay ahead for him. He had a fair bit of information already from his doctors, but hearing about it from someone who actually went through it all put his mind at ease a bit more.

Oisín went on to make a full recovery, returned to inter-county football and won an Ulster championship medal with Cavan in 2020. He scored two points in the final against Donegal, helping them to their first provincial title in 23 years, so I was absolutely delighted for him.

Helping somebody through the process is always something I am willing to do, and I find sometimes it actually helps me as well.

It's just a nice thing, and what I'm here for really.

GOING BACK TO 2018, as the dust settled on the county title with the club, life returned to normal at work. But the well-wishes never really stopped.

People were full of admiration for me in terms of coming out on the right side of things twice and working in healthcare myself, on top of winning that medal at 47.

In 2018 I didn't play any football and just helped out with Castlerahan, and Aughnasheelin survived being back in senior football thanks to a relegation play-off victory over St Patrick's Dromahair.

I was up and down to Cavan two or three times a week to train the goalkeepers, and they won their first ever county title that season.

They repeated the dose in 2019, but Aughnasheelin weren't so lucky in Leitrim and went back down to intermediate football after suffering relegation that year.

WE HAD A 'Leitrim 1994' reunion at the 2019 Connacht final in the Galway Bay Hotel to mark the 25th anniversary of our victory and we were presented with pieces of Galway Crystal to mark the occasion. We were also guests of honour at the Leitrim county final, with a gala dinner that night in Carrick, which also happened to be my birthday.

Seeing all the lads was wonderful, and after some catching up, the stories started and lots of the old craic came back to life again.

I have all of the games from that summer recorded and I watch them back the odd time.

They're all on YouTube now too, if anyone wants a good laugh at the grainy old footage from when Leitrim made history.

It's amazing when you look back on those matches at just how poor we all were, compared to the athletes that inter-county footballers are now. If you watch the start of our Connacht final win over Mayo, we kicked the ball away and gave away a daft goal.

But if an inter-county manager asked a panel today to do the training we had to do, they'd be laughed at. We had no physios, no specialised coaches and no big backroom teams like they all have now. It's changed times and that's the way the game has gone. But mentally, we were hard as nails and had the fitness to outrun Mayo, and that's what happened on the day. It's nice to look back at it, because we made history and nobody can take that away from us.

And let's call a spade a spade, that will probably never happen again in my lifetime so it was nice to reflect on what we achieved with the lads again too.

It was great craic reliving those old glory days with the boys – some of whom are in great shape, while a few of the rest of us have put on a few pounds. We're all really looking forward to the 50-year reunion in 2044!

Despite everything that life has thrown at me since then, that Connacht championship medal is like gold-dust to me.

So many great players will play inter-county football for years and put in the same effort, but sadly they will come nowhere near a senior provincial title. It's something we'll have until we're six feet under.

It's something we'll have forever.

Epilogue

*The 25th anniversary celebration of our Connacht championship win
was an emotional and memorable day for all of us who helped make
that amazing day in the history of Leitrim GAA happen.*

« EPILOGUE »

EVERYDAY I LIVE now is a good day. I've gone from strength-to-strength at work, and relish looking after patients who are unwell.

Many of them are suffering with dementia which is another incredibly real and sad condition which can really stop you in your tracks. But I always try to put a smile on someone's face every day. Paddy could be 90 and not want to eat his dinner, but I always try and have a bit of craic with him to coax him into eating.

The other extreme could be someone who is really going through a hard time after having a stroke or a heart attack.

Watching someone's condition improve every day is a powerful thing, especially when you see them leaving the hospital to go home. That's what it's all about.

Such a huge effort goes into everyday life in a hospital, between doctors and nurses to save lives, and there is nothing like watching someone else make a full recovery – and I help them in every way possible to do that as well.

OBVIOUSLY, THERE IS another side to it, and some days can be stressful and exhausting. You could be pulled from pillar to post to all sorts of different jobs and you are juiced by the time the day is over. It's a hugely rewarding job and it's very enjoyable.

I just love working in the hospital and in tandem with that, football always provides me with that little lease of life to get off my ass and go and do a bit of training or play a game when I'm away from the job.

But more off the field drama was about to unfold, and this time it swept the globe. The Covid-19 pandemic brought the whole lot to a halt in 2020, and that really highlighted the huge part football and sport plays in our lives, because it was taken away.

Harsh lockdowns with no training or matches were one thing, but people were dying and we had to deal with that on the front line at work.

When the virus arrived, everyone was really worried because this disease was killing people… everyone was terrified. At the start, we were totally in the dark and hospitals were really struggling to deal with the chaos of it all.

I was in the thick of it no more than every healthcare worker across the globe, and everyone really went above and beyond during what was nothing short of an emergency, especially when it first arrived.

We had to gown-up in full protective equipment for everything, especially during those first few months of 2020. There was always a question over who has the virus and who doesn't in those initial weeks and months, and gowning-up in fresh PPE constantly can be an awful pain in the backside.

You have to wear a special large mask, goggles, apron, a full gown, booties over your shoes and a hair net every single time you go near a patient to give yourself and them as much protection as possible.

It was a pain, but it had to be done to protect ourselves and others, because at that point there was no word of a vaccine or any sort of a cure. We were very much in the unknown, and it was frightening.

We had special wards for Covid-only patients, and when you went into regular wards you still didn't know if it had spread there too, because you can't see the disease and you really had to walk on egg-shells.

You could be working in casualty and things were separated there too, with a green area for patients clear of the virus and a red area for those who had it or were showing symptoms.

Nobody was coming into the hospital any more with minor issues but some patients who caught Covid were seriously ill and brought to the intensive care unit, and that was surreal.

You would have other people turning up and answering 'no' to all of the Covid protocol questions because they wanted to be seen, but they were actually carrying the virus into the hospital, putting a strain on services and putting everyone at risk.

We had instances where someone would be waiting in the green area of casualty with regular problems, and someone else would be near them coughing and spluttering, and who would test positive for the virus.

They would have to go straight to the red area, and it meant everyone else who came in virus-free would have to be tested as they were deemed close contacts, including the staff.

During the whole thing it was infuriating at times seeing the heroic work in the hospital from all of us… cleaners, kitchen staff, porters, security, and nurses and doctors – and then hearing about people not adhering to the guidelines or even going abroad when the virus was really taking over the whole world.

It was really draining going to work when the virus was at its peak, and then you had people out there who didn't even believe it existed and said it was all a hoax.

It was terrifying seeing people with the virus lying in intensive care in critical condition, hooked up to machines and ventilators, and we regularly had to move those patients on to their sides or their backs to keep blood circulating as we were covered from head to toe in PPE.

And even with all that protective gear on, staff were still coming down with the virus and at times things descended into chaos, which made it a very tough environment to work in.

It was always in the back of your head that anyone could have it, from patients to your fellow staff, as you went about your day. We had to treat everyone as if they had Covid-19.

Patients were picking the virus up without even leaving their beds, which was also terrifying.

It was gruelling dealing with the pandemic every single day when it was at its peak and it seemed like it would never end, but the vaccines are working well and, thankfully, there has been a huge uptake here in Ireland.

People are still getting sick after having their jabs, but they aren't getting seriously ill which is a good thing. We probably just have to live with it now and hope that the variants get weaker, and normality will eventually return.

It was physically draining and very mentally demanding on all of the staff for every single second of every day. And astonishingly, we still have to remind people to wear a mask and wash their hands when they come in. It really highlights that some people just don't care, and that's a fact.

I ENDED UP catching the virus myself, but not until August 2021, and thankfully by then the vaccines had arrived and I had received my two doses.

As a frontline worker, I was jabbed up early and that meant I wasn't seriously ill, but I would not like to have picked up the virus without the vaccinations I had.

I picked it up at work doing some regular chores with patients when one of them contracted the virus, and any staff who had been in that particular ward had to be tested. I've done enough of them now, but the PCR tests are not the most pleasant experience when that long swab goes up your nose.

I got a phone call that night to say I was positive, and my heart dropped.

On top of that, I was so angry after taking so many precautions after nearly a year and a half – and yet a regular patient in a regular room infected me and five other staff members in the one go.

I had no symptoms at all but it meant I had to self-isolate for 10 days at home, and as I went to bed that night I could feel a chill creeping through my shoulders. I paid no heed to it as I had been sitting beside an open window, as it was the summer, but as the night went on I gradually started coughing and a few aches and pains filtered through my body.

The chills came at me again, and when I woke the next morning, I felt tired and weak as the cough worsened – that was the start of it, and I really knew then that I had it.

As the day went on, I got worse and started to panic, because I presumed it was going to be all downhill from here. On top of that, I was worried it would affect my lungs because they are already weak from going through chemotherapy.

I was sitting on the armchair feeling as weak as water when Linda suggested I take a drop of poitín. As a staunch Pioneer, I was immediately against her suggestion. I had never drank through all of the football celebrations I was lucky enough to be part of, and could have easily turned to alcohol during my cancer ordeal.

I was hardly going to start now.

I knew I'd be as well off drinking diesel, because it's seriously strong shit but she swore it would help, and I eventually gave in. She filled me a good hot glass of it with some water and sugar.

The smell of it was rancid and the taste was worse, but eventually I got it into me over the course of 20 minutes or so. I could feel the sweats coming on me then, and when I woke the following morning, I was even worse again. I had no energy at all, and just went from the bed to the toilet and back again.

When I made it to the sofa at one stage, I just fell asleep on it. I was killed with aches and pains and the constant coughing.

I was so bad because of my underlying health conditions. I had visions in my head of calling an ambulance. I didn't want to go that far, but I was preparing for the worst.

Linda came back at me with more of that horrific poitín, and I told her where to go with it but I eventually gave in. This time, she put a dash of blackcurrant through it to soften the harshness of the taste of that devil juice.

I drank it down and it did taste a bit better, but it wasn't enough to pull me off the wagon and hit the drink by any means.

I even had another glass of it, and by 10.30pm I was conked out in bed for the night. I woke at around 4am and the bed was drenched in sweat – after cleaning myself up a bit I cuddled into a huge winter duvet and drifted off again.

I still had some symptoms the next day again, which was Monday by then, but I felt a good bit better than my two previous days. As the day went on I could feel myself coming around. I even made it out of the house that day and spent some time in the garden, and that evening I was close to normality. I was so relieved to be over the worst of it, and dreaded the thought of what it would have been like to catch the virus before I'd been vaccinated.

I know people out there will not take a vaccine, but it has saved lives and I would have been in a serious condition without the protection they gave me.

I ADORE MY job, but you always have to expect the unexpected because I got the virus doing my work.

The pandemic evolved all the time. At the start it was chaos and no more people were arriving with simple things like a sore leg or a bee sting because they were afraid to come near the place.

As the months went on and the restrictions loosened up a bit, people started coming back to the hospital with those minor problems. But what is very frustrating from our point of view is that every day the hospital is struggling with staff numbers and people are coming in with problems that their own doctor would be able to sort out for them.

The pressure in the hospital from the accident and emergency department, to every ward, right to the intensive care unit is immense, and every person that comes in with a small problem intensifies that pressure every single time.

The funny thing is, if a patient comes in with a cut on their hand that needs stitches, they could wait six or seven hours to be seen, whereas if they went to their GP the wait time would be a fraction of that.

2020 and 2021 in particular were really hectic because staff across the board in every hospital were burnt out with the same routine every day, and people with minor problems coming in or calling an ambulance for trivial problems as others were seriously ill, were really piling pressure on everyone.

Covid aside, my work can be so rewarding and there are a lot of great, heart-warming stories that I've witnessed on the job.

I had been having banter with a patient I knew one morning and gave him a shave and a wash and some fresh clothes, and he asked me if I could put a drop of poitín into his water! Sadly, I didn't have any of Linda's stuff with me that day.

Those were some of his last words, and a few minutes later he was gone. He started to slip away in front of me, and died in my arms.

It's heart-breaking when that happens, but it's part and parcel of the job. Someone can come in and just go downhill and pass on.

You try not to get too emotionally attached, but you do build up relationships with your patients naturally when you see them a few times a day... and that goes on for weeks, months or even years.

You can relate to what they are going through, and they love having someone to talk to – especially when the pandemic was at its peak. During that time, they could have no visitors, which was incredibly tough for people who had to endure illness or require constant care in the first place.

Suddenly, they had to go through it on their own without seeing their loved ones, and the staff in the hospital were all they had. They could be having a very bad day and feel very ill, and sadly you can be a front row spectator when they fail to recover and pass away.

That's just the sad reality of life sometimes and it is what we have to deal with all the time in the job.

Another patient we had suffered a heart attack on his farm, and we had to keep an eye on him constantly in case he fell out of his bed. He was a Leitrim man, but we struggled to communicate with him because of the pain he was in. After a day or two, I told him I was Martin McHugh from Aughnasheelin; I could see him cracking a smile and even producing a little giggle despite how ill he was.

He seemed at ease in my company, and later in the day we hoisted him out of his bed and into a chair, but he was clearly very uncomfortable and restless. Another day when nobody was looking, myself and one of the nurses tried to see if he could stand up, because he was making gradual progress.

So, we slowly helped him to his feet and, sure enough, he was standing there with our support as a big smile beamed across his face. He still had a long way to go, but it was a huge day for all of us because the fact that he wanted to walk was just incredible.

The next day I managed to take him for a few steps and gave him a shower and the smile returned, but he still couldn't talk. Towards the end of my shift, I told him I was going home and to behave himself until I would be back the following week. He grinned again, and was able to verbally thank me as I left.

About six weeks passed and he improved with each day, as his voice gradually got stronger. Watching him return to health like that was really astounding. *And guess what?* He is now back at home, fully recovered and working on his farm!

He is jumping gates, working with his animals, driving around in his tractor and behind the wheel of his car, which is truly remarkable.

That is one of the many good stories from life in Sligo University Hospital, though you try and keep it all light-hearted and good humoured to get through each day no matter what comes at you.

I just love caring for people. I love going in and leaving again after a 12-hour shift knowing that I gave it my all that day to help people and look after patients.

THE PANDEMIC DID see my grá to play football come roaring back again, even though my body had been waving a white flag for so long, and sure enough I went back playing as I turned 50 in November 2020!

I'm still going, and I still know full well my playing days are coming to an end, but it's just great to be back at it again.

In 2021, I played a few league games with Aughnasheelin again before Kevin McWeeney volunteered to play in goal. Kevin has traditionally played outfield, but time is catching up with him too – and when he put his hand up to try life between the sticks I said, 'No better man!' It was time to let him in there so he could learn.

I still enjoy going to training and getting phone calls from clubs to come in and help their goalkeepers. It's great heading off in the car to hand down my knowledge to some young goalkeeper looking to make a mark.

Life on the GAA front is good, even if Linda is telling me to stop playing football! She wants me to hang up my gloves and my boots and every other bit of gear I check meticulously for, but she can wait.

I'm well aware that I'm nearly 52, and not 32 anymore but I'm going to stay involved in the GAA for as long as I can, because you are long enough outside the wire looking in.

If I'm driving around at night and see a set of floodlights somewhere, I'll head over to see what's going on just to watch whoever it is go through their paces at training or playing a game.

Football is my oxygen and my drug, and it saved me when I thought my life was going to end.

It gave me so much discipline to look after myself, and if I didn't have GAA when I was diagnosed with testicular cancer in 2009, I probably would have died and would be pushing up daisies right now. It's a scary thought, but I think it's the truth.

Before I had cancer, I was going through a tough marriage separation and between juggling work, football and everything else I failed to look after myself.

I'd be pulling and dragging at something every day and that stemmed from when I was a young lad at home chopping wood, pulling calves, lifting bales of hay and working on the bog before training and going to bed.

Hard work was all we knew, but I think that stood to me because it helped me develop a physical and mental toughness.

But looking back on my adult life, I was stressed to the point where I was hit with an atomic bomb in the form of testicular cancer and the chemo and thoughts of death that came with it.

I knew after all of that, I had to change my attitude and had to start looking after myself. I promised myself when things settled down, that's what I would do… and I have stuck to that rigorously.

My football career was resurrected, and it opened up a path towards an unlikely career in healthcare which I have loved every minute of.

YOU NEVER KNOW what's around the corner, and those blood tests I have every six months to keep an eye on things are vital.

Touch wood, everything so far has been okay, and if anything ever does crop up and something is wrong, I'll be ready to hit it on the head and beat it again. And If I'm told things are looking bleak and I have months to live, I'll attack the bucket list and tick off everything on it.

I'd love to go on a cruise, and when I turned 50 in 2020, we were meant to go on one but Covid ended that plan. Doing a parachute jump for charity is on the list too, and there's always other little mad ideas running through my head all the time.

There's no point sitting and living on the edge worrying about everything either, so I just enjoy every single second of each day and will stick to that mantra until my time comes.

I love going to the schools and colleges and whoever else will listen to me to tell my story. I know people going through what I went through myself, and I'm their Dr Phil – I'm their therapist and they quiz me on this, that and the other… and I'm able to answer them.

We are all on this earth for a reason, whether that's helping out a football team or being there for someone who has been told they have a serious illness like cancer.

When I heard John O'Mahony had been diagnosed with multiple myeloma cancer in 2020, I sent him a message of support and told him I was there for anything he needed. He's doing mighty now; positivity helped him through it and he's even back in management with the Salthill-Knocknacarra club in Galway.

I've been living in Geevagh village in Sligo with Linda, near where the county borders with Leitrim and Roscommon. There are lots of lakes and rivers around Geevagh, and Lough Allen is only down the road so there is lots to do in the area. and I can go fishing as I please whenever I want to switch off.

It's nice and quiet, but there's always a bit of gardening or work to be done too! We are only 20 minutes from Aughnasheelin and 20 minutes from Sligo town where we both work, as Linda works in the hospital too.

Because no visitors were allowed during Covid, she would bring things up to patients that are dropped in, or take patients arriving for appointments to their clinics. We are a mighty couple, and she has been my saving grace too because she was there when I was sick the second time and helped me through it every single step of the way.

We have been very happy since; she keeps manners on me and life is good. We are off work at weekends, and Linda loves going to my football games and has turned into a real pundit when the post-match analysis has to be done.

Life now is based around enjoyment – whether that be spending time with Linda and the rest of my family, working in the hospital, playing or coaching football... or getting good news from my blood tests every six months.

I live life to the full and take each day as it comes.

In a past life, when I was stressing out every day about all of the jobs I had to do, and trying to juggle too many things at once, I ended up with cancer twice and I can't lose sight of that.

Now I just get out of bed and enjoy the day... rain, hail or shine. There is no point worrying about silly things.

I work because I enjoy it, and the same applies to everything else – whether it is giving talks about my experiences or playing football. I still prepare for the worst, but always hope for the best. That's all you can do.

At work we have patients from all over Sligo, Roscommon, Mayo and Donegal and the surrounding areas. But I always try to have that extra bit of banter with someone if they're from Leitrim.

Often when I say who I am, they remember I was the goalkeeper who played football for the county. Amazingly, you still get the odd person who will want to shake your hand and call you a legend for winning that Connacht title.

The odd time I wouldn't tell them who I am at all, and I would suss out if they knew their football or how good their memories are.

'That was a great Leitrim team we had in 1994,' I would say, and their faces would light up and the floodgates would open with chat. They might mention Declan Darcy – the captain who went off to play for Dublin. They might talk about Seamus Quinn, the great full-back who won an All Star.

Their faces might fill with joy remembering the team that beat Galway,

Roscommon and Mayo – and getting all the way to Croke Park to take on Dublin in an All-Ireland semi-final, with the genius John O'Mahony managing them.

Then, I would ask them for the craic about the buck who played in goals? And they'd have a think for a second in silence before the reply.

'Oh yeah… the small fella! From Aughnasheelin!'